POWERFUL PROOF

POWERFUL PROOF

Personal stories of God's powerful
presence in our lives

LINDA HACKENBRUCK

outskirts
press

Powerful Proof
Personal stories of God's powerful presence in our lives
All Rights Reserved.
Copyright © 2025 Linda Hackenbruck
v3.0

The opinions expressed in this manuscript are solely the opinions of the author and do not represent the opinions or thoughts of the publisher. The author has represented and warranted full ownership and/or legal right to publish all the materials in this book.

This book may not be reproduced, transmitted, or stored in whole or in part by any means, including graphic, electronic, or mechanical without the express written consent of the publisher except in the case of brief quotations embodied in critical articles and reviews.

Outskirts Press, Inc.
http://www.outskirtspress.com

ISBN: 978-1-9772-7560-8

Cover Photo © 2025 www.gettyimages.com. All rights reserved - used with permission.

Outskirts Press and the "OP" logo are trademarks belonging to Outskirts Press, Inc.

PRINTED IN THE UNITED STATES OF AMERICA

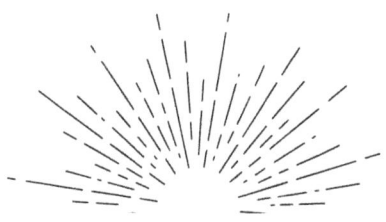

To my husband, Jerry, who has shared God's love and miracles with me.

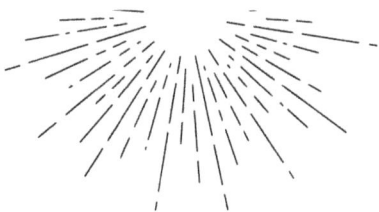

Contents

INTRODUCTION
Powerful Proof ~ i

ONE
Meeting Jesus and Learning to Trust ~ 1

TWO
An Ugly Couch and God's Provision ~ 8

THREE
His Incredible Love in a Dishwasher ~ 13

FOUR
A Child's Prayer ~ 19

FIVE
Miracle Job ~ 23

SIX
Seeking His Will in Worship ~ 31

SEVEN
Please Let Us Keep Her ~ 42

EIGHT
My Mother's Shooting Star ~ 57

NINE
Forgiveness Times Four ~ 70

TEN
Covered With Prayer ~ 85

ELEVEN
In His Time or Never Give Up ~ 97

TWELVE
Only One Tail Light ~ 107

THIRTEEN
Miracle of the Black Angel ~ 121

FOURTEEN
The Legal Fiasco and Faith ~ 145

FIFTEEN
Never Ending Houses ~ 169

SIXTEEN
Devastating Loss ~ 196

SEVENTEEN
One More House: Julie's Prayer ~ 217

EIGHTEEN
The Light and the Love ~ 223

CONCLUSION
From the Heart ~ 229

Acknowledgements ~ 232

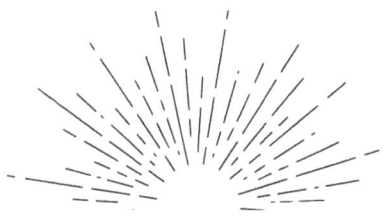

INTRODUCTION
Powerful Proof

Personal stories of God's love and miracles.

These stories are about my relationship with God from age three through the decades. I began writing them in obedience to the urging of the Holy Spirit fifteen years ago. My prayer is that the loving nature of our living God will be revealed to you in a life changing way.

I've gone from a three-year-old who believed Jesus loved her to a woman who truly loves the Lord my God with all my heart, soul, mind and strength. God has taken me on a journey of trust that has led to His will for choosing my spouse, the size of my family, giving up my desires and receiving more than I asked for, a medical mistake that led to cerebral palsy for my baby, how to forgive, twenty-four moves in thirty-two years, cancer, death of a child and seeing Jesus. I have learned that God's most important love lessons are learned in pain and suffering and if given to Him, they will be turned into joy and peace.

Each time we as a family humbled ourselves and turned to God as the Father He is and trusted Him to teach us, meet our needs and help us with our lives, He revealed Himself to us in a mighty way. He showed Himself as a Father who is interested in the details of our lives as well as the big picture. We learned that He is waiting to bless and teach us if only we will turn to Him in trust and give Him the chance. We found that He always surprises us and gives more than we know to ask for. He delights in a humble heart because it is a teachable heart and He is truly our Father and we are truly His children.

God is Father of us all. He cares about us and our life situations. He created us to love us, if only we will let Him. As a follower of Christ, it is so very frustrating to see how Christianity and God are viewed in our time and culture. Jesus came to reveal the Father and reconcile us back to Him. He did nothing but love us every day of His life all the way to dying for us on a cross. He revealed a Father whose love for each of us is beyond comprehension. God sent the Holy Spirit to connect us straight to His loving heart each and every day of our lives. Many individuals struggle with belief in Jesus, God the Father and the Holy Spirit. Some have asked why I believe and how I can be so sure God is real. I tell them I know God is not only real but is lovingly involved in my everyday life. I tell them the absolute truth as I have lived it. Here are my true stories. They are my powerful proof of an intimate, loving, trustworthy God.

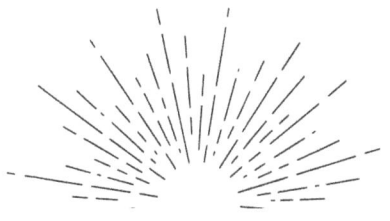

ONE

Meeting Jesus and Learning to Trust

We are never too young or old to talk to Jesus and hear Him talking to us.

I remember smearing Vaseline on my black patent leather shoes when I was three years old. The Vaseline made them shiny and pretty. I had to get from the front door of our house to the car door without stepping in any dirt because we all know what happens when dirt hits Vaseline. Next was getting from the car to the door of the church, again without stepping in any dirt. That's what I remember most about going to church as a child; that, and singing Jesus Loves Me in the Children's Choir. I sang Jesus Loves Me and I believed it.

My family was like many others in the 1950's.

My parents brought five of us into the world in seven years and if my Nana hadn't bought us clothes and toys for Christmas, we wouldn't have had any. I knew not to ask for anything and I never did, that is until the day I saw something I just had to have.

It was early December and I had just turned four. We were all together at the dime store, ages: six, five, four, almost one and not quite born. I remember standing at the glass case staring at Him. I couldn't move. I didn't want to look at anything else. I knew inside of me that I had to have Him. I was afraid to ask my mom but I wanted Him more than I was afraid. I mustered up my courage and when Mom came to find me, I asked her.

"See baby Jesus? I want Him."

I watched her face and the expressions that crossed it. First there was no way, we can't afford it, it's not necessary. Then she studied me and softened. It was really important to me; I never asked for anything and there it was; she cared about me. She opened her purse and bought Him. I carried Him home but I really carried Him in my heart. He sat in front of the little church decoration each Christmas, but he really sat smack dab in the middle of my life. I talked to Him, prayed to Him, told Him my troubles and my secrets.

There was a lot of strife in our home because my

mom was mentally ill and my parents were not well suited to each other. Jesus became my childhood confidant. I leaned on Him when fighting broke out between my parents or my mom and siblings. I couldn't stand the awful words and the violence. I disappeared in Jesus and looked for ways to bring peace to our home.

When I was nine and ready to start the fourth grade, we moved to a new town. My dad was hired as a teacher and basketball coach. It was a good opportunity for him and my Nana lived there so I was pretty excited until I started school. I was used to having lots of friends in our old town but the kids at my new school didn't seem to like me. All of our belongings were packed in storage for the first week of school because we couldn't get into our new house, so I had to wear the same dress every day.

That was bad enough, but to make things worse my mom had decided that 'her' girls were going to wear saddle shoes (the white and brown ones that she wore two decades before) and start a new trend in our new town. I don't and never will know why she decided that but we absolutely couldn't cross her. My two sisters and I begged her to let us get something in style, but saddle shoes it was. Saddle shoes were popular in the 1940's and this was 1963!

I was very lonely at school. I ate lunch by myself and hid in the play shed watching the girls in my grade run around together. After a few days of this, I walked home at lunch time and told my mother I wasn't going to school any more. She chased me out of the house threatening to spank me and told me to get back to school! I was truly empty, frightened and in despair as I walked back to school. I remember going inside myself to find God for comfort. I asked Him to please help me at school.

The next day at lunch time I got up all my courage and walked up to a group of girls from my class. I asked if I could play with them. The ringleader of the group started whispering to the others and then they laughed and all ran away. I was devastated. I had taken a chance and they had rejected me. I walked outside the play shed and started to cry. That's when God intervened for me. One girl left the others and walked back.

"I will play with you," she said.

One was enough, more than enough for me. I stopped crying and thanked her and we played the rest of recess. After that experience, I had friends and I also had more compassion for hurting people. Even as a nine-year old, God was using daily life experiences to teach me His ways and mold me for

His use in the future.

Something else happened that fourth-grade year that would change the course of my life. I was walking single file down the hallway coming back from P.E. class. We walked past the fifth and sixth grade classrooms to get to our room. I noticed a boy sitting on the floor outside Mr. Cole's fifth grade classroom. I felt a strange shock go through me. It was a tingling sensation travelling from my head to my toes and it was the first time I felt the Holy Spirit getting my attention. I was a shy, afraid to do anything wrong, never boy crazy kind of girl, but I had to turn around and take a second look at this boy because something about him was important that I didn't understand. The boy saw me turn around and look at him and he made a horrible face at me. I continued back to my classroom with my face burning up with embarrassment. I prayed he wouldn't remember me if he ever saw me again but I continued to watch him around school, on the playground, on the bus, with other girls, at the skating rink, baseball games and anywhere else I ran into him.

In the sixth grade, my sister and I were laying on our beds upstairs looking out our window and talking when the boy walked by on the sidewalk below. I told my sister that I would never marry anyone until I had a chance to date Jerry Hackenbruck.

She laughed and said, "Oh yeah."

There is much more to this story, but eleven years later I married that boy. I know God pointed him out to me at the age of nine. I was in tune with God and had learned to listen to His voice. We are never too old or too young to talk to Him or hear Him talking to us.

My family had stopped going to church by the time we moved to this new town, so I started setting my alarm and walking to our neighborhood church alone when I was ten. I loved God and I did what I thought would please Him. When I was eleven, I asked Him to help me quit doing two things. One was to quit eating potato chips. I could eat a whole bag at a time and somewhere inside I knew that was going to hurt me. The other was to quit saying critical comments about people. Every time unkind words came out of my mouth, I felt ashamed. I didn't seem to be able to control my mouth, so I asked God for help. As the months passed, potato chips had no hold on me. I refused them easily. My mouth was harder to control, but over time God gently cut off the destructive words. My friends started noticing that I was quiet during gossip and commented about how nice I was and how I never said anything unkind about anyone. I was learning what grace was and to who the glory belonged. My faith was building from experience with a real, living God.

At age seventeen, I was attending Young Life at my high school and I experienced fellowship with other believers. I was no longer alone in my faith and it was powerful. I needed spending money at this point in my life and still didn't ask for anything at home, so I turned to God. I was sitting on the grass all alone and I asked Him to help me find a way to get money. Later that day I stopped by my boyfriend's job at the grocery store and he introduced me to one of his coworkers.

"You wouldn't want a part time job, would you?" she asked.

I got chills all over. Of course, the job which was working as a nanny and doing household chores, was exactly the right hours for me. She wanted me to start right away and the pay was decent. That was the first time I brought a practical need to God and he answered quickly in a mighty way. That was the first time and this book is about the times that followed. He has proven Himself real, faithful, wise and loving to me one hundred per cent of the time. God is real, He desperately cares and He has proved it.

TWO

An Ugly Couch and God's Provision

As I surrendered my will and repented of my sin, He gifted to me much more than I could ever have acquired on my own.

The ugliest couch in the world sat in our tiny living room, but no one ever sat on it. The wood floor was more comfortable. My husband and I were married while we were still in college. We lived in married student housing and it came furnished except for our bed and our baby's crib and dresser. When my husband got his first job, he immediately bought us a house which turned out to be a brilliant financial move. At the time however, I was a little panicky. The house payment left us with no disposable income. We had an eleven-month-old baby and another one on the way, one car that barely ran, and we had no furniture. As we left married student housing, heading to our first home, we bought a dirty beige, vinyl couch at an auction for ten dollars. It was actually a couch bed so we now had a place for company to sleep. We thought we had gotten a steal. The fact was no one else wanted it. They probably knew that couch beds are extremely heavy and awkward to move and even worse to sleep on. We didn't. We were also unaware that this particular couch was very uncomfortable to even sit on. Everything sank toward the middle. We were twenty-two years old and naïve in the ways of furniture.

After three years of looking at our awesome purchase, I started thinking of ways to get rid of it. But how was I going to justify a new couch when we had no money and we had a viable couch, however ugly and uncomfortable? I glared at that couch every time I walked by the living room. I placed a blanket on the back of it to improve the appearance but it did nothing for the problem of sitting on it. I gave myself pep talks about how wonderful it was for our two toddlers to climb on and how they couldn't hurt or ruin it. That didn't help.

My husband was coaching football and we were hosting an upcoming after game party. I became obsessed with how ugly the couch was and how much better our house would look if we could just replace it. After letting my mind focus on the couch long enough, I started talking about it to my husband. I told him all the reasons we needed a new couch. He loved me so he listened. He knew the couch was ugly and uncomfortable and he wanted to make me happy.

One day he came home and told me about a weekend job he could take on the side to make more money so that we could afford a new couch and other things for our family. He was serious. I was shocked. We were expecting our third child and he was willing to take a second job to give me the "things" I wanted. I immediately felt ashamed before God. We didn't "need" a new couch. We didn't need it for comfort, or for a party or for any reason at all. We certainly didn't need it more than my children needed their daddy home to play with them! I told my husband that I didn't want a new couch that badly and I would never give up time together for a couch or any other material thing. Then I went to God in prayer and I asked Him to forgive me for causing my husband to feel bad about his provision for us. I asked forgiveness for my pride in the appearance of our home, and for coveting material things. I told Him that I was done complaining about that couch and I really was. It quit bothering me and believe it or not our after-game party was a lot of fun and people sat on the couch, all sinking toward the middle!

Shortly after my prayer of repentance, my father was hired as basketball coach for the college in our city. My mom and dad moved over the mountain and bought a home in our neighborhood. We were so excited to have them close. On moving day, my husband went over to help them move things in while I stayed home with the little girls and cooked dinner for everyone.

Later that day the door opened and my husband came in and said,

"How would you like to have a new couch?"

This wasn't just any couch; this was our favorite couch! It belonged to my parents and it was unbelievably comfortable. It was extra-long with a high back and rolled arms with pillows to lie against. It was covered in a brown tweed fabric that hid dirt. It could seat four people comfortably and was amazing to sleep on. I absolutely couldn't believe it. If we had bought a couch, we wouldn't have been able to afford or to find a couch like theirs.

"Why are they giving us their couch?" I asked.

"They didn't want to give it up but it won't fit into their basement," he said. "The stairs going down to their family room has a turn in it and they couldn't make the couch fit through that turn. There was nowhere to put the couch in their house."

Later that day, my parents arrived with the couch. It went right through the front door and fit perfectly along the wall that looked out toward the front picture window. It went perfectly with my wallpaper, paint color, and curtains. It changed the look of our living room and made it feel cozy and inviting. It was heavenly to sit on.

God had done it again. As I surrendered my will and repented of my sin, He gifted me with much more than I could ever have acquired on my own. He gave me my favorite couch in the world; the one my heart really desired; the one I couldn't have attained by my own devices. God showed His great love for me again but the real blessing in my experience of the couch was not receiving the couch. It was learning the deeper lesson of what is really important in this life. It is not material things and appearance or even comfort. It is loving one another, choosing time together over things, and trusting God with all our needs, even couches.

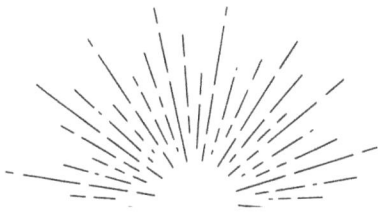

THREE

His Incredible Love in a Dishwasher

When I gave up my "rights" and trusted God with what was "right" for me, He showed me His amazing love and blessed me as only He knows how.

Our second house came with a dishwasher. It was old, ugly, and dirty blue. It didn't match my red and green apple kitchen. It was big and portable and had to be hooked up to the faucet at the sink. When it was hooked up and running, it blocked the walk-through space in the small alley kitchen but I was excited because I had never had a dishwasher. I loaded it up, plugged it in and it washed those dishes. I loved having a dishwasher.

When our third baby in less than four years

was born, our house was busy, busy, busy and I was tired, tired, tired. One evening I loaded that dishwasher up to the brim, hooked it up to the sink, pulled out the starter knob and nothing. I pushed the starter knob back in, checked that the water was on, pulled the starter back out and nothing. I kicked the darn thing in the side, pushed the knob in, pulled it out and nothing. After getting our two and three- year- olds to bed and with the baby in the front pack, I unloaded the entire dishwasher of dirty dishes to the counter, filled up the sink, washed them, dried them and put them all away. I was exhausted when my husband came home from work after nine o'clock that night. We were extremely short on money but he said we could get the dishwasher fixed.

 The next morning, he called an appliance repair technician who came out two days later. I saved all the dirty dishes on the counter until the machine was fixed. The technician spent about 30 minutes in the kitchen and gave me a hefty bill. I wrote him a check and he left. I was so excited. I loaded up all my saved dirty dishes, turned the big heavy machine around to the sink, hooked it up and pulled the knob. Nothing. I tried again. Nothing. When my husband returned home, I was in tears. We had paid for a repair with money we really didn't have and the dishwasher still didn't work.

HIS INCREDIBLE LOVE IN A DISHWASHER

My husband helped me unload the dirty dishes to the counter, wash them, dry them and put them away. While we worked, I told him just how much I needed a dishwasher with three small children. I told him that I thought it was truly a need vs. a want at this point in our life and asked if we could try and fix it again.

He called the technician who came right back the next day with a fifty-dollar part for the dishwasher. He said that this would fix the problem for sure and he replaced the old part. It was hard to give him fifty more dollars, but I did and he left. I couldn't wait to try the dishwasher again. That evening when the toddlers were asleep, I loaded up all the dirty dishes. I pushed the machine around, hooked it up to the sink and pulled the starter knob. Guess what? Nothing. This couldn't be happening. I had just paid $50 that we didn't have to fix a dishwasher that I thought I couldn't live without. The guy said it would run for sure. It had to run. I tried it again and nothing. I sat down and admitted defeat.

"OK, Lord, I give up," I said. "I'm through. There must be some reason that I am not supposed to have a dishwasher. Maybe You have a different plan. Do You want me to pray each day while I wash the dishes? It could be a fun time for me and the two little girls to wash dishes together. People got along without dishwashers for thousands of years. There is no real reason that I need a dishwasher. I'm finished trying so hard to have a dishwasher. I am never going to complain about not having a dishwasher again and I will not ask for one either." Then I threw out my challenge.

"If You want me to have a dishwasher, You will need to bring one to me." And that was that. Later that evening I told my husband that I had decided I didn't need a dishwasher and he could call the repair technician and get our money back. I unloaded all the dirty dishes, washed them, dried them and put them away. I was totally at peace and filled with an amazing joy instead of frustration over what I thought I deserved.

A few days passed by and I washed dishes. The little girls played in the water standing on chairs and helped rinse and I held the baby in the front pack. We did just fine. I was happy and forgot I needed a dishwasher.

Within two weeks of my prayer, surrender and challenge to God, there was a knock on the front door. I opened the door and there stood Uncle Woelfle. Uncle Woelfle is my husband's best friend from high school and our second child's godfather. I hadn't seen him in over a year. He didn't say hello when I greeted him. He didn't ask if my husband was home or if he could see the new

baby. He looked kind of confused.
"Do you need a dishwasher?" he asked.
I was completely taken aback.
"Do I need a dishwasher?" I answered shakily.
"Yes", he repeated, "Do you need a dishwasher?"
I still couldn't believe what I was hearing so I just stood there and stared at him until he continued.
"I have a dishwasher that I don't know what to do with and I started wondering if you needed one."
"As a matter of fact, I do need a dishwasher."
I told him the story of our defunct dishwasher and about how I had told God that if He wanted me to receive one, He would have to bring it to me.
"Where is your dishwasher?" I asked.
"I have it in the van,"
"You have it here?" I asked incredulously.
"It's in the van. I'll bring it in,"
He hauled the dishwasher into the kitchen and guess what? It was new. It was a beautiful green color that perfectly matched my red and green apple wallpaper. It had a cutting board on the top that I could actually use as a work space.
Uncle Woelfle told me that he had to move suddenly out of a house and didn't want to leave his new dishwasher there, even though he had nowhere to put it. He said he had no idea why he had brought it to our house, except that as

he was driving down the I-5 freeway it popped into his head that Jerry and Linda might need a dishwasher. He turned off the freeway at our exit and drove straight to our house. I offered to buy it but he wouldn't even think of taking any money for it. He just sincerely wanted us to have it.

I knew why he brought that beautiful dishwasher to our house. Uncle Woelfle was listening to the prompting of the Holy Spirit. God was teaching me to trust him. He wanted me to have a dishwasher, and not just any dishwasher. He wanted me to have a new green one to match my kitchen with a cutting board to increase my workspace. He wanted me to have it for free. He wanted me to have the best. When I finally gave up my "right" to a dishwasher and trusted God with whether a dishwasher was "right" for me, I allowed Him to show me His amazing love and bless me as only He knows how.

Over the next six years, we brought home three more babies to our little house with that wonderful dishwasher. It helped give me more time to care for our children, but more importantly, it gave me an increased faith in God's presence in my daily life and his ever-present love for our family.

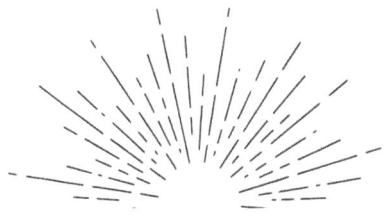

FOUR

A Child's Prayer

*I was trying to control her faith with my fear.
He asked me to put away my fear and trust Him
with my daughter.*

After our experiences with the dishwasher and the couch, my faith was growing by leaps and bounds. Christmas season had rolled around and our local high school was having a Christmas pageant. Each princess in the pageant was to choose a child to be a little princess with them. Our three-year old daughter Heidi was chosen as one of the little princesses. My husband came home and told her that a very nice high school girl had chosen her to be a little princess. She was beyond excited.

Heidi was to dress up in a long red or green dress, walk into the assembly with her big princess friend, and sit on the stage. There was only one problem.

She didn't own a red or green dress, let alone a long one. We were still living paycheck to paycheck. We couldn't buy any extras because we didn't believe in using credit cards. We lived within our means, period. I told Heidi that we couldn't afford a new dress but she could wear one of the dresses in her closet and it would be just fine.

"Why don't we ask Jesus for a new dress? He can get it for me," Heidi said with confidence.

OK, I knew what God could do for those who asked and trusted Him, but I had only taken my own problems and needs to Him, not my children's. I felt the old fear enter in. Here came my doubts, my lack of faith. I was afraid to ask Him for a dress for my daughter. What if He didn't deliver? What would that do to her faith? I went to Him in prayer. As I talked to God, He reminded me that He was responsible for Heidi and her faith and that I was trying to control her faith with my fear. He reminded me that she was His child and that He loved her. He asked me to put away my fear and trust Him with my daughter... His daughter.

I found Heidi and asked her to pray with me. We told God that she needed a long red or green dress for the Christmas pageant at the high school. We told Him we didn't have a long red or green dress and we didn't have the money to buy one. We asked Him to bring her a long red or green dress before the pageant. We said thank you and Amen.

She was happy and I made every effort to fight my fear. I tried to stop myself when I would start thinking of ways to buy her a dress. I thought of all my family and who I could call and ask to buy a dress for Heidi. I looked in her closet at her three not so nice dresses and tried to figure out how I could change them or fix them up. I was still trying to control and play God. I could give up things for myself but I was totally struggling when it came to my children.

The days went by and the pageant was getting closer. Heidi didn't say anything more about her dress and I didn't either. Then one afternoon, two days before the pageant, we came home from the grocery store and saw something on the front porch. There were two brown paper bags. We brought them into the house. They were full of clothes, children's clothes; girl's size four and five. On the very top of one of the bags was a long dress. It was a size four, Heidi's size. It had a white puffed sleeve bodice with green embroidered Christmas trees on it. The skirt was green with thin white stripes and it had a red tie. It was beautiful and of course it fit perfectly.

"Jesus brought me my dress!" Heidi shouted.

I cried tears of joy.

We found out later that an acquaintance had decided to clean out her daughter's closet and thought of us because we had two little girls just younger than hers. She left the clothes on the porch hoping our girls would like them. Heidi and I knew why she left them on that day. She thought of us because her little girl had outgrown a long, red and green Christmas dress. Heidi needed that dress and she had taken that need to Jesus.

I learned on that wonderful day that Jesus didn't belong only to me. He belonged to my children, too. He was big enough for all of us and I needn't be afraid anymore.

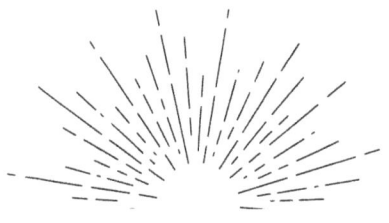

FIVE

Miracle Job

"But seek first his kingdom and his righteousness, and all these things will be given to you as well."

Shortly before the birth of our third baby my husband was offered a new job. He was in his third year of teaching high school and he coached football, basketball and track. We had a small, two-bedroom house and one old car that broke down regularly. I shopped for groceries with a strict budgeted list, used coupons and bought no paper products other than toilet paper. It drove my mom nuts that we never had napkins on the table. I used baking soda for deodorant, we kept our thermostat at 64 degrees in the winter and we all wore sweatshirts (our guests kept their coats on). We didn't buy any clothes and we never made it through a month. I cut everything I could think of out of our budget and was still writing checks for groceries at the end of the month that wouldn't clear the bank before our paycheck did. We didn't go out to dinner, to movies, vacation or even go to potlucks when we didn't have money for ingredients for a salad or casserole. I started worrying about money.

My husband was smart, handsome, positive, funny, humble and an all-around great guy. People liked him instantly. He had a Business and Marketing degree as well as a Master's degree in Education. The parent of one of his students was an executive for Blitz-Weinhardt brewing company in Portland, Oregon. He needed a new marketing manager for his company and he approached my husband about taking the job. Our teaching job paid $12,000 a year. This marketing job came with a salary of $25,000 a year plus (and this was the biggie) a company car. This meant that not only would we be able to pay our bills and buy food, but we would have a second car, paid for with free gas and insurance.

My husband told me about the job offer and I told him to take it. He said we should pray about it. I told him to take it. He said he wasn't sure it was where God wanted him to be. I told him to take it. We prayed together and I told him to take it. He said we should keep praying and wait for direction. I prayed that he would take it. We talked about it again and I told him how much the extra money and a car would help me. I told him that one of the children could have an accident and I wouldn't be able to get them to the hospital because I never had access to the car. I told him how sick I was of trying to make ends meet and how I couldn't find any more ways to save money. I told him how happy it would make me to be able to buy presents for people and to be able to pay for a gym class for our three-year old. I told him I desperately needed a new maternity top!

He listened and then he told me he was sure God wanted him to stay in teaching and coaching. He said that God would use him to help young people in the schools and that was more important than making more money. I told you he was a great guy. He turned down the marketing job with the big salary and the car.

I was frustrated and disappointed. I had already imagined my life with a car. I had imagined actually shopping for clothes for my children. I had imagined turning up the heat in our house. I went to God and told Him in no uncertain terms that my husband was wrong and that we needed that money. We didn't just want it, we needed it. Didn't Jesus say not to worry about money because our needs would be met? When did food, clothes and heat become non-needs? I prayed to God to help me with this disappointment and to show me that He really was leading my husband.

A couple days later when I had cooled down, I talked to my husband about my conversation with God. I told him that our needs weren't being met and I couldn't cut any more corners in our budget. My husband said that he knew we needed more money and that he would look for a second job. Everything in me screamed "No!" In three-months we would have a new baby. We would also have a three-year old and a two-year old. My husband already coached three sports a year and was almost never home. Another job? He had to be kidding me. I went back to God. I prayed and looked up the passage in scripture that spoke about our needs being met. I found it in Matthew 6:31-33:

> *"So do not worry, saying 'What shall we eat?' or 'What shall we drink?' or 'What shall we wear?' For pagans run after all these things, and your heavenly Father knows that you need them. But seek first his kingdom and his righteousness, and all these things will be given to you as well."*

OK. I knew I wasn't supposed to worry but I had forgotten the part about *first* seeking His kingdom. My husband was obviously seeking His kingdom and I thought I was seeking His kingdom, but I was really worrying about money. I did remember the scripture about how you can't serve two masters, God and mammon, and I really didn't want a lot of money; I just wanted to make it through a month!

After I read the passage in Matthew chapter 6, another one on the page caught my eye. It was Matthew 7:7-11, the one about Ask, Seek and Knock.

"Ask and it will be given to you; seek and you will find; knock and the door will be opened to you. For everyone who asks, receives; he who seeks, finds; and to him who knocks, the door will be opened." "Which of you, if his son asks for bread, will give him a stone? Or if he asks for a fish, will give him a snake? If you, then, though you are evil, know how to give good gifts to your children, how much more will your Father in heaven give good gifts to those who ask Him!"

I took God up on his promises. I told Him that I wouldn't worry about money, but instead I would trust Him to provide our needs. I also told Him I would ask for His help. I then went to my kingdom seeking husband and shared the scripture verses with him. We discussed what our "needs" truly were and decided that we needed money to meet our basic physical needs, time to meet our children's needs and we needed time together as a family. We asked for the impossible. We asked God for both time and money. We asked sincerely and with expectant faith. I have to admit I was still wondering about that new job we turned down. I also was curious to see if God could really deliver.

We prayed our prayer in March and I kid you not we got a call within three days! Forty-four years later, I still can hardly believe it. God gave us time and money! An acquaintance of my husband who worked at the high school across town ran a swim park during the summer. His assistant had just resigned and for 'some reason' my husband had popped into his head as a possible replacement. This swim park job paid $4000 for the summer. Each director would work only half the days of the summer and guess where the swim park was located? It sat only two blocks away down the hill from our little house. There was a walking path, maintained by the city, across the street that took us straight down there. So basically, I didn't need a car to get to my husband's job at a swim park where we could spend every minute with him.

MIRACLE JOB

The park had a baby pool with a sand area that was enclosed with a fence and it had benches for parents to sit on and watch their children. It had a climbing structure for little ones and a bathroom building and a snack bar. It had picnic tables and barbeques so that we could bring lunch or dinner down to eat together as a family on the days my husband worked and he only worked *half* the days! We could walk up home for naps and come back to play with Daddy for the evening. The swim park job came with a bigger salary than any other summer job possibility we had heard of. We were dumbfounded and gratefully accepted the job. We joyfully thanked God for His love and providing for our needs.

Of course, there were more blessings to come from the answer to our prayer. Our children all learned to swim for free at that park. The oldest three eventually had summer jobs there with schedules that allowed for family time for the next fifteen years. I met some of my best friends there while we sat around the baby pool or on blankets under the trees. I met other mothers whose children were playing with mine. We shared food and stories about our children and our lives. This sharing sometimes led to faith stories and we would teach each other and build each other up.

God had again proved to us that He was real,

that He cared deeply about our family and our willingness to serve Him. He proved that He would meet our needs. True to form, He gave much more than we had asked for. We had asked for time and money. We received them both and we also received new friends, playmates for our children and a wonderful setting for our little ones to grow and play in. Because we asked Him, believed in Him and trusted Him, He showed himself to be real and faithful. He met our needs and our joy in living life with Him overflowed.

SIX

Seeking His Will in Worship

Jesus prayed for us to be "one" in Him; to be "one" in our love. To fulfill His prayer, we have no room to judge or condemn another's faith. Our life work is to love and be one in our love.

When I was little my parents were afraid one of us would grow up and marry a Catholic. I was the one. I never understood the anti-Catholic thing. My friends who were Catholic seemed just like me. We went to Young Life in high school together and we worshipped the same God. When I was sixteen, I started dating my husband and I started going to the Catholic church with him. My family didn't go to church and I liked going with him rather than by myself. His church didn't seem so different to me. I had grown up going infrequently to the Episcopal church and the Catholic church had the same service format and tradition. I received good teaching during those high school years attending mass as a non-Catholic and sharing our time at church was great for my husband's and my relationship.

Eventually, we were married in the Catholic church because it was important to my husband and we were growing in our faith in Christ there. I will never forget the message Father Charles Harris gave to us. He told us to spend the rest of our lives trying to out serve each other. We listened and we took it to heart. If two people are always trying to out serve each other, how can they ever be disappointed or want to leave? I have read many marriage books over the years, but nothing has helped my marriage anywhere near as much as that humbly given sermon by Father Harris.

After our second child was born, I took classes and joined the Catholic church. I wanted our family to worship in one faith and I was growing in my faith there. We spent much of our time at mass in the "Cry Room" because the church didn't have a nursery for babies and toddlers. I met other mothers with strong faith in the Cry Room and they became my close friends.

While I was pregnant with our third child, a friend invited me to a nationwide Bible study that was taught at the Presbyterian church just down the road from our house. The Bible study was non-denominational and had a children's program. I was very excited for the chance to learn more about the words of the Bible and I joined. I loved it! I soaked up everything I could learn about scripture. I did each weekly lesson, took the Bible to heart, applied it to my daily life and memorized scripture like crazy. I loved being in God's word. As I studied the lessons over a two-year period, I became more and more aware of anti-Catholic sentiment hidden or sometimes not so hidden in the lessons. The empty tradition and sinful history of the church and the buildings full of people going through the motions of religion without knowing God became repeated themes.

I started to question the Catholic church's tradition and formal services. I started to feel bitter that my children didn't have a Sunday school program. I began complaining to my husband about our church and how I wanted something more for myself and our children. He encouraged me to pray about it and listen for God's voice. I went to my small group leader at Bible Study and talked to her about my confusion about Bible Study and my church. She said maybe God was trying to tell me something and I should pray about where He wanted me to be.

I did pray and God told me in no uncertain terms to stay in the Catholic church. This is what happened. The Sunday after I talked to my small group leader, we went to mass and I got down on my knees and prayed. I said a simple, earnest prayer.

I prayed, "God, show me a reason to stay."

Mass went on as usual. When mass was over, my husband and I and our three little ones got up to leave. As we reached the aisle and turned toward the door, a lady came pushing her way through the crowded aisle toward us. She seemed a little frazzled and was definitely heading somewhere in the opposite direction of the crowd. Suddenly she stopped right in front of me.

"I need to talk to you," she said.

I had never seen this lady in my life and was a little taken aback.

"OK," I answered.

I followed her out of the crowd. When we were alone, she told me that she had been praying before mass about starting a young mother's group. She felt the young Catholic moms needed to get to know one another and pray together. She said as she was praying, God pointed me out to her and told her to go talk to me. She said she would be happy to host the group at her house and that children would be welcome but she needed me to help her invite mothers to come. God certainly answered my prayer, "Give me a reason to stay." I was right where He wanted me but He wanted me to help start a young mother's group and pray with other Catholic women and grow with them. I told the precious lady about my prayer before mass and we both knew that God had brought us together. Soon we had a mother's group up and running. God used my experiences in the "Cry Room" because that is where I met most of the mothers who joined our group.

But God didn't stop there. One of the moms who joined our group belonged to a charismatic prayer group that met Sunday evenings in the Parish Hall. She invited me and my husband to come with her and her husband to the prayer meeting. We went and had wonderful worship in the form of music, prayer, teaching and sharing. The people in the group were baptized in the Holy Spirit and used the gifts they had received to build up the body of Christ. I didn't know much about the Holy Spirit, the third Person of the Trinity, but I am pretty sure He had been with me and teaching me as a child. I started praying to Him with Jesus and God the Father and I found that my love for all people grew at an amazing rate. I had a joy I had never known possible. My husband grew in love and devotion to God as much or more than I did. We rarely missed a prayer meeting even though we needed a babysitter to go. We made the closest friends we'd ever had because we all shared such a deep faith. We helped and loved one another's families. It was such a blessing to be in that Catholic prayer group and God wasn't done teaching and blessing us there.

    My husband started having severe back trouble. He'd had a neck injury playing football in high school. The injury was so bad that he was paralyzed for a short time and spent a few days in traction in the hospital. He recovered and played football through college, never complaining about the pain he endured because he loved the game. Now we were twenty-six and his back was getting increasingly worse to the point that he couldn't sit or stand very long. He was definitely not a complainer but I found him lying on the floor, flat on his back in various rooms of the house. He went to the doctor and was put in bed, on his back to rest it for a week and then reassess. It was no better. He was headed for surgery.
    We went to a prayer meeting and someone

asked my husband why he was standing rather than sitting in a chair in our circle. He shared that his back was so bad that he needed surgery very soon. The group asked if they could pray over him for healing. He said sure but I could tell he was a little uncomfortable because we weren't used to prayer for healing. They put him on a chair and some of our group laid hands on him and started to pray. I will never forget what I saw. My big football player husband, all two hundred twenty pounds of him started jerking on that chair. He jerked so hard that he started falling off onto the floor and the leaders caught him. His face was filled with awe and he could hardly speak. He told the group that he had felt electricity go through his body and settle in his back. He had felt a warmth go through him. His back was pain free. He received healing from God through the Holy Spirit and the healing lasted years before it flared up again. Our faith and knowledge of who our God was and what He could do was increased.

Shortly after this I was approached by another member of our parish who was commissioned to start a preschool program for Sunday mornings. I ended up teaching one of the classes and had input into the program that blessed my children and others in the parish. God showed me that He didn't want me to complain about what our church didn't have but to get in there and help make good things happen.

I had continued attending Bible Study during this time of growth in the Catholic church. I enjoyed the lessons but still felt uncomfortable with some of the anti-Catholic sentiment. If God had kept me in the Catholic church and He definitely had, He must love and sanction it as well as the Protestant churches. I found out through a close friend who had joined the leadership at Bible Study that they had written rules in their doctrine that Catholics and divorced women couldn't join the leadership team. I was disillusioned with this "nondenominational" group.

I went to Holy Week services leading up to Easter and found our church packed each night. I wondered if all churches were packed nightly during that week. I thought about my dear friends who had suffered devastating divorces through no fault of their own and how much they leaned on the Lord and loved Him. I didn't feel comfortable at the Bible Study any more.

We were studying the Gospel of John that year and we came to Chapter 17 at the same time I was feeling uncomfortable. John 17 consists of three prayers that Jesus prayed right before he went to the olive grove where he was arrested to be put on trial and crucified. The first prayer Jesus prayed was for Himself, the second for His disciples, and the last was for All Believers. It was this last prayer that struck me as ironic to be studying at Bible Study where Catholics and divorcees had rules separating them. I want to share with you John 17: vs. 20-23:

> *"My prayer is not for them alone. I pray also for those who will believe in me through their message, that all of them may be **one**, Father, just as you are in me and I am in you. May they also be in us so that the world may believe that you have sent me. I have given them the glory that you gave me, that they may be **one** as we are **one**: I in them and you in me. May they be brought to complete **unity** to let the world know that you sent me and have loved them even as you have loved me."*

The Bible Study leader made the point in her lecture on this scripture that it was a shame that the Church had become so corrupt that it had to break apart during the Reformation. I don't question the corruption but I do question the breaking apart. It broke the oneness of God's people. They turned their backs on Jesus' prayer for them. The

Catholic church is still standing as are Protestant denominations. Corruption still shows up because sin is real. His people worship in different churches and settings but His true faithful are still one in their love of Him and each other.

    I grew up loving God with my whole heart. I trusted Him with my life and my decisions. When I sincerely and trustingly asked him where He wanted me to worship, he told me to stay in the Catholic church. I was committed to obeying His will to the best of my ability. I have stayed in the Catholic church.

    Each of us has our own relationship with God. He loves us all and has an infinite number of ways to reach us. He will lead us where He wants us to go if we seek His will. He prayed for us to be "one" in Him. Jesus prayed for us to love one another as He loved us. To fulfill those prayers, we have no room to judge or condemn another's faith. Our life's work is to love and be one in our love. This is why my eyes gloss over and my ears go numb when people start to argue denominations or bash Catholicism. God kept me close to Him in the Catholic church. It is where He taught me to follow Him each day. I found the Holy Spirit in the Catholic church; my husband was healed in the Catholic church and I made some of my strongest Christian friends in the Catholic church.

Which brings me to the end of Jesus' prayer for all believers in John 17: vs. 25-26:

> "Righteous Father, though the world does not know you, I know you, and they know that you have sent me. I have made you known to them, and will continue to make you known in order that the **love** you have for me may **be in them and that I myself may be in them.**"

He said it all. His last spoken prayer for us (other than for forgiveness from the cross) was that we would be one and that God's love would be in us and He himself would be in us. That prayer lets us know as Christians, we will be known by our love and we need to pray for unity of all true believers.

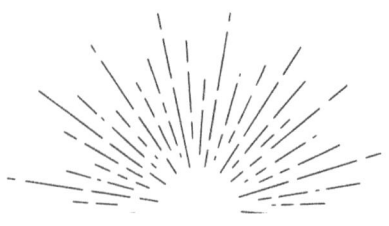

SEVEN

Please Let Us Keep Her

Father, we know Julie belongs to You. You created her and gave her to us and We thank You for her. Today, we give her back to You.

We danced in the garage. We held hands, circled, danced and cheered. The Goodwill truck pulled out of the driveway taking eight years of my life with it. Four-year old Joey asked, "Mommy, who is good Will?" Laughing, I told him Goodwill wasn't a person but an organization who would give our baby things to other families. No more babies for us. Into the house we danced to continue our celebration with lunch.

My twenties disappeared in a blur of babies. I was grateful to God for the four children he had blessed us with, but was ready to move on. My husband and I had a clear plan. We would both teach and have time together with our family. While still at Oregon State University, our first baby was born, followed by three more. Our youngest turned two and I registered for fall classes to finish the last semester of my degree in Elementary Education.

Classes started in August. By June, I was pregnant again. Were we idiots? How could this have happened? It wasn't like we didn't know how babies were made. We had tried everything available and still ended up pregnant. I loved God. I wanted to do His will and bring Him glory, but four children was enough. My husband was a teacher and coach so his income was set. We had no bonuses or family money to fall back on. We were barely able to live within our means and had no discretionary income. How were we going to raise and educate five children on a teaching salary? What was God thinking? We prayed together, rededicated ourselves to God and gave Him our trust concerning the size and raising of our family.

We didn't share our baby news. We savored the new life and love growing inside me. Violent retching became the story of my days. The veins in my legs distended and made roadmaps down to my black and blue ankles. Even though I was miserable, I did love the baby and that love became my focus. Our children were ecstatic to have a new baby coming and their joy helped me cope.

Jennifer, our seven-year-old, begged God every night, "Please let Mommy have twin girls."

My silent prayer, *please don't*.

The pregnancy was soon noticed. I was rapidly showing. Being my fifth pregnancy, it kind of made sense but by four months I was starting to fill out my maternity clothes. The vomiting had subsided, only to be replaced with an extremely itchy red rash that covered my body. I scratched until I bled. If I woke up at night, I would feel the itching move through my body and in the mornings, I cried because I was awake and had to live through another day. Anything against my skin made me miserable so I wore huge silky caftans. I kept the house at 64 degrees because heat would increase the intensity of the itch. It was a living nightmare. Something was wrong in my body. I needed medical help and I wasn't getting it from my doctor.

My baby was due on February 13. I arrived at my prenatal appointment on December 23 armed with a list of concerns: I could no longer get maternity clothes over my stomach that I had worn with nine-pound babies; I could feel hiccups at the small of my back and hold onto a little foot at the top of my tummy; I was losing mucous daily and having sharp pains at my cervix. I told my doctor, as I had at the previous three appointments, I suspected twins. I asked for an ultrasound. He told me to lie down, tape measured my stomach, stated I was *not* having twins and refused me the ultrasound. After my twins were born, I read an article that listed the symptoms of premature labor, the exact symptoms I had taken on my list to my doctor when he sent me home to take care of four young children.

On Saturday, January fifth, my emotions were raging. It was like I had PMS times twenty, bad enough to get my husband's attention. By evening, he decided we were going to the hospital in the morning. The older girls went with us.

We arrived and checked in for an exam. I laid down and felt a light contraction. The nurse checked my cervix. She quickly headed for the door.

"Where are you going? What's wrong?" I called anxiously.

She looked back over her shoulder and answered, "You're ten centimeters and ready to deliver,"

My husband and girls were excited but I was scared. The baby was 5 ½ weeks early. Our other children had all been on time and something was wrong. I willed the contractions to stop. I was not ready for this baby. I asked God to help me. The nurse came back into the room and took me straight to delivery.

In the delivery room, I was told to push at the slightest contraction. On the second push Julie Christine was born. The doctor held her up and she turned her head to look around the room. She was beautiful, looking exactly like her brother Joey.

"That baby is too small. Is there another baby in there?" I asked.

Julie was five pounds four ounces, over three pounds less than any of our other babies. The doctor reached inside me.

"Yes, there is another baby," he answered.

The room broke out in pandemonium. More help was called in. We all waited for another contraction. I pushed hard and Molly Kathleen was delivered. The doctor held up the still intact water sac and I could see her inside, a view I will never forget. When her sac was broken, Molly's legs and arms flew out and she started to scream. I wanted to comfort her but wasn't allowed to hold her. She weighed two pounds, fourteen ounces, was all skin and bones, no extra fat, no hair and her fingernails were transparent. I was in shock and scared. The babies were scooped up and taken to the Neonatal Intensive Care Unit. My husband and daughters followed, with Jennifer jumping for joy that God had answered her prayer for twin girls.

PLEASE LET US KEEP HER

It was an hour after my babies went to the NICU that I saw them again. Molly was in an incubator and doing amazingly well. She was breathing on her own. Julie, was under an oxygen hood and her little chest was heaving with each breath. She'd had almost perfect APGAR scores after birth, seven and nine. I was supposed to worry about Molly, not Julie. I was wrong. The nurse assigned to the girls explained that Molly had been in distress in utero because her cord was marginally inserted into the placenta. Very little food had reached her, barely enough to live. Her lungs had developed quickly because of the distress. Julie had plenty of food inside and grew steadily. Her lungs had no reason to develop quickly and therefore they still needed help. That made sense to me at the time, but I read later that if preemies get chilled after birth, they can develop a breathing problem. Julie was strong, holding her head up and had breathed perfectly for fifteen minutes in the delivery room. When Molly was discovered inside, Julie had been laid naked in an open bed. She wasn't even wrapped in a blanket. I kept looking over and asking if she was all right lying there all alone. She may have chilled while waiting for Molly and had a breathing problem by the time she got to the NICU.

Late that afternoon, the pediatrician in the NICU wanted our permission to put an umbilical artery catheter in Julie. This procedure would allow blood to be drawn through the catheter to check her oxygen and carbon dioxide levels. I didn't know what the procedure entailed so I asked him if it was safe. He told me it was standard procedure. The nurses encouraged us to have the catheter placed. They told us it would be best for Julie, so we agreed. What they didn't tell us was the pediatrician wanting to do the procedure was not a neonatologist. He was rotating through the nursery on a double shift, had been working long hours and Julie's heel could just be poked to draw blood. The experienced neonatologist would be on duty early the next morning and she could do the catheter if it was needed.

While I was back in my room, the pediatrician put the catheter in. My mother was watching through the nursery window. Julie was screaming throughout the procedure. I got up a few times in the night to check on my babies and Julie was very agitated. A nurse was fiddling with her catheter when I came into the nursery and I asked if something was wrong. She said that she was just making sure it was in the right place. I couldn't sleep.

Early the next morning, I went into the NICU to find the actual neonatologist examining Julie. The doctor looked really angry.

The nurse immediately said, "This is the baby's mother."

The doctor nodded to me and quickly left the nursery.

Julie's catheter had been inserted incorrectly. The pediatrician had not secured it in place and by leaving it free to move around it could move from the umbilical to the connecting renal and aortic arteries. Julie looked terrible. She was puffing up with fluid and her skin had become all mottled during the night. I asked what was wrong and the nurse told me Julie was still fighting to breathe and it was good she wasn't on a respirator. She didn't tell me the neonatologist had discovered Julie's left kidney had hemorrhaged. Julie was in renal failure.

That afternoon I was standing by Julie's open bed praying over her when she had a full body seizure. Her entire body lifted up off the bed, her arms and legs flew out stiff and she collapsed back down on the bed. I called to the nurse who yelled for the doctor. Julie wasn't breathing and her heart had stopped beating. She looked different. Her muscle tone had gone weak. Her arms and legs were floppy and her features had changed. The nurse started CPR and the doctor put Julie on a respirator to breathe for her. While this was happening, a different nurse tried to take me to Molly, but Molly was doing just fine. I was staying with Julie.

Looking back, I think my husband and I were in shock. Our "one" baby wasn't even due and we had two babies. Julie was obviously not doing well, but we couldn't quite take that in. We stayed by the babies in the nursery, talking and singing to them and touching them. My husband didn't get any paid time off from school and we needed his salary, so he went back to work the next day. I spent every minute I could in the nursery with the babies. Molly was doing well, but Julie was getting more mottled and swollen. I felt helpless.

Early in the afternoon, when the twins were two days old, the nurses took me back to my room to get off my swollen legs. I lay down in bed and the neonatologist arrived. He wanted to talk to me about Julie. He informed me that Julie had been catheterized for twelve hours and no urine had been drawn. Her kidneys had completely shut down. I asked him what we could do to start them again. He said dialysis was an option but not a very realistic one on a preemie baby. She couldn't live on dialysis long enough to get strong enough for a kidney transplant. Julie's kidney failure had opened a grade three (meaning big) hole in her heart from the pressure of the extra fluid in her body. Her lungs were weakening, fighting with her heart, making it unlikely she would ever breathe on her own and her brain had been damaged by the seizure she had sustained. He said that Julie was dying and that I should call my husband to come to the hospital. He said our children needed to come also, scrub down, put on gowns and masks and go into the NICU with Julie. It was important for her siblings to touch their sister before she died. After Julie died, he said her father and I would be able to hold her for as long as we wanted to say good bye. Then he asked me if I had someone I could ask to go buy an outfit to bury Julie in. I told him that my mother would do that. As he was leaving the room, I asked him if there was any hope. He told me there was always hope.

I said, "We will hold onto that hope."

I called my husband's school, asking them to send him to the hospital. Julie was dying. My mother was bringing the children.

As I sat in shock, a lady entered my room carrying papers. She introduced herself as a social worker and had brought in autopsy papers for me to sign. She proceeded to tell me that she had watched many autopsies and just how respectfully they were done. After our baby died and we had spent time with her, she would be taken somewhere in the hospital for an autopsy to discover what had caused her kidneys to shut down. As I listened to her my anger grew. My baby was alive. I had not given up hope that she would somehow continue to live, and this social worker wanted me to sign autopsy papers as if her death was a done deal. With anger and disbelief, I told her that my baby lived, we were praying for her and we were not giving up on her. I told her that I was certainly not going to sign autopsy papers for my living daughter, my children were coming to see their sister and I would like her to leave the room. She turned on her heel and left without a word.

My husband, mother and children arrived at the hospital. The children couldn't wait to see and touch their sisters. We told them Julie was very sick and we wanted them to talk to her and tell her how much they loved her. God made Julie and she belonged to Him and we were hoping she could stay in our family. We were going into the NICU together to pray for her. Our four little ones scrubbed down, put on gowns and masks and we all entered the NICU. We pulled Molly's incubator over next to the open bed Julie was laying on. Julie had tubes coming out of her and she was on a respirator that was taped to her mouth. She was swollen and mottled. The children touched both babies and told them that they loved them. Julie's appearance didn't faze them. She was their sister, just as she was. They reached into Molly's incubator to touch her and held Julie's hands and feet as they gifted their sisters with their precious, familiar voices.

We wanted to baptize Julie, so my husband got a glass of water and we all surrounded her bed. Laying six pairs of loving hands on her, I prayed aloud a simple prayer:

"Father, we know Julie belongs to You. You made her and You gave her to us and we thank You for her. Today, we give her back to You because we know You love her even more than we do. But if it could be Your will that we keep her, in any condition at all, we ask You to let her stay. Thank you."

We all said, "Amen," and put our trust wholly in God.

My husband said, "Julie Christine, we baptize you in the name of the Father and of the Son and of the Holy Spirit. Amen."

He poured the water over her head.

When we left the NICU nursery, my mother was waiting outside for us. She looked shaken and was trying not to cry. I asked the nurses if she could scrub down and go in with me to see Julie. They said that she could, so we went into the NICU together. My mother had many struggles in her life but love was her gift and she loved little Julie. We went over to Julie's bed and my mother talked to her for a while. I spent some time with Molly so Mom could see Julie alone. I asked Mom if she would like to pray for Julie with me. She said that she would, so we laid hands on Julie and started to pray. Just as we began, a little stream of very bloody urine shot out of Julie. Her right kidney had kicked back in and was starting to work. My mom and I stared in disbelief. I called the nurse over and she was very excited. It was about twenty minutes since we had asked God if we could keep her.

After that miraculous moment, Julie had a hard fight ahead of her to live. She had to overcome damage to four of her five major organs: brain, heart, lungs and kidneys. We knew for certain that she would make it because God had answered our prayer and was going to let us keep her. I spent fifteen hours a day in the NICU with Julie and Molly. I talked and sang to Julie while I held Molly. When Julie was about a week old, we finally got to hold her. It was a magical moment and she snuggled right into me. The nurses let me bathe her and she opened her eyes for the very first time in the water. I think she thought she was safe, back inside the womb. Her eyes were beautiful and making eye contact with her was amazing.

PLEASE LET US KEEP HER

Eventually, Julie was unhooked from all the machines and the nurses put her into a bassinet bed with Molly. The girls immediately snuggled over to each other and Molly threw her arm over Julie as if to say, *Sister, where have you been? I've missed you.* The more we held and sang to Julie and the more time she spent with Molly, the faster her recovery became. The doctors had said that she would probably spend three months in the NICU but she came home at five weeks of age, only two days after Molly.

When we got home with the twins, we started noticing a beautiful light that shined out from Julie's face. Her eyes shined bright and light reflected over her entire face. Other people started noticing it, too: family, friends and strangers out in public. She shined with that pure light throughout her preschool years. We were always convinced that she had seen God and the light we saw was His lingering presence. We had simply asked Him against all odds if we could keep her and He had said, yes. He had left His light shining in her so we would know that she was His gift to us and what an amazing gift she was!

God has blessed our family through Julie. All the children are kind and in helping professions.

Her sister Jennifer loved playing with Julie and teaching her new things. She is now an occupational therapist. Julie's identical twin sister, Molly, decided to become a nurse and work in the NICU where she could make sure no babies were hurt like her sister had been. After graduating with a Bachelor of Science in Nursing she applied for an open position in the NICU at a Portland hospital. Calling me right after the interview, she told me she had been hired on the spot. The head nurse on the interview committee had taken care of Julie and Molly when they were born. She remembered every one of our children and my husband and me. The nurses had known that Julie was dying and they had watched our family pray over her. They knew that they had witnessed a miracle when she lived. They never forgot Julie and Molly and the family that trusted and prayed to a God who loved them.

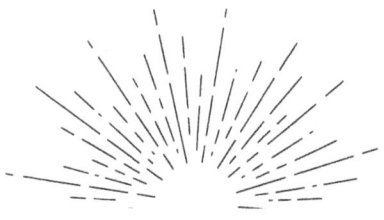

EIGHT

My Mother's Shooting Star

God remembered the little girl who had suffered so many years with worry about her mother. He had been with her, feeling her pain.

I loved my mother. She was the most beautiful person in the world to me. I thought she looked like a movie star, only prettier. No matter how much I loved her, tried to please her and make her happy, I couldn't. My mother was mentally ill. She probably had bipolar disease and narcissistic personality disorder, but her illness wasn't diagnosed. That was common when I was a child growing up in the fifties and sixties. People didn't talk about mental illness and they certainly didn't admit to it. We all pretended she was OK because that was what we were supposed to do. Nobody told us to pretend but we all knew that was what was expected.

POWERFUL PROOF

When I was two years, eight months old, I watched my mother try to kill my father. I was standing in our dining room with my sisters, ages five and barely four. My parents were in the dining room near the opening to the kitchen. My mother was screaming and stabbing at my father with a butcher knife. Four months later, at just three years of age, I was very sick and diagnosed with a serious ulcer. That was also the year I found Jesus and his love for me. I talked to Him every day for the rest of my life.

I woke up every morning listening hard. I would listen for my mother and the sounds she was making: chairs being pushed softly against the wood floor or shoved into the table or wall, her voice laughing, talking to someone on the phone or angry sounds, yelling or crying. Anything could set her off and I spent my days trying to run interference with the world around her to keep her happy. I was called "Little Peacemaker" by adults and "Miss Perfect" by my siblings.

I watched my mother save animals and nurse them back to health, give to the less fortunate, read us dozens of books, play the piano and sing for us, rock and sing to the babies, do ten loads of laundry a day, and stay up all night to make one of us a dress for a dance. I watched my mother beat my six-year-old sister with a belt for playing with her cowboy boots, hit my five-year old sister hard in the back every time she coughed and hit my dad in the head with a spike heel until blood squirted out.

My mother attended everything I ever did and everything my siblings did. She was always sitting in the crowd smiling at us. She drove us to practice, games and everywhere we needed to go. She drove our friends too, when their parents were too busy. She was very dedicated to us and involved in our lives unless she was preoccupied with her own pain. Then she was hard to reach and forgetful.

At times, my mother lied about where she went in the day and evening. I needed her one day and rode my bicycle to her job at the bookstore. She was on a break so I went to the nearby coffee shop and saw her holding hands with a guy that was not my father. He was the father of a boy in my junior high school. One day the boy came up to me in front of my friends.

"I hear your mother knows my father," he said with a chuckle.

I was horrified, said I didn't know anything about his father and walked away. I knew my mother must be having an affair and I tried to avoid that boy from then on.

POWERFUL PROOF

The Friday I had my wisdom teeth pulled, I was laying on the couch in pain, spitting out blood, when my mom walked into the room all dressed up and smelling strongly of perfume. She said that she was going for a drive. I couldn't believe it. I really needed her to get ice bags and help me. When she left, I felt so helpless and sad. I knew she wasn't just "going for a drive." A few days later my mom and I were at my best friend's house.

My friend's mother said, "Steve (her husband) has been acting so strange lately. Friday night he left and went for a long drive by himself. He needs a lot of time alone lately and I'm worried about him."

Of course, Friday was the night my mom went for her long drive alone. When my friend's mother was talking, Mom quickly looked at me to see if I was putting it together. Yes, I was and she looked really scared. When that affair ended it made my friendship uncomfortable and caused future problems for me and my friend.

My mother loved getting dressed up and going out. She loved make up, jewelry and perfume. To this day I can still smell her perfume. My dad didn't take her out very often and I felt sorry for her. During the spring of my senior year in high school, the school voted for prom court princesses. I didn't know anything about it and didn't vote. One of my friends came up to me at a party.

"Linda, you're on the prom court," she said.

"Oh, now my mother can go to the prom!" I replied.

The first thing that came out of my mouth on hearing about the prom court was, "Oh, now my mother can go to the prom!" How weird was that? I didn't care about the prom court, but I knew that parents of the princesses got invited to come to the prom. I knew that this was a chance for my mom to get dressed up and go out. I knew this would make her happy. For a few hours it probably did. I still didn't know I couldn't make her or anybody else happy. I didn't know happiness had to come from within. I didn't know that only God could heal my mom and give her the joy inside that she so desperately needed. But I kept trying for thirty-one years and then something happened.

I gave birth to our twins Julie and Molly and Julie got hurt in the hospital nursery. She was dying and my mom and I prayed over her for healing. Julie lived and my mom's faith was born. She told me she began praying every day in the shower for Julie and that she really got to know God.

POWERFUL PROOF

After the twins turned one, my husband was offered a head football coaching job in the town where my parents were living. Our children were nine, seven, five, three, one and one and I was so happy at the prospect of my mother's help. My mother did love my children. We moved.

About two weeks after we settled into our rental house, my mother was diagnosed with breast cancer. She was fifty-five. I was thirty-two. She had a mastectomy and had lymph nodes removed from under her left arm. Cancer was in nine of the thirteen lymph nodes, a death sentence for sure, but I didn't know it. She fought the cancer for two years undergoing chemotherapy and various medications. The cancer spread to her bones, liver, lungs and brain. She lived with constant nausea and pain. She had to stop doing many things she loved because she was too weak or her brain couldn't remember how to do them. The day she could no longer play the piano was a very sad day.

We did everything we could think of to keep her comfortable and show her that we loved her. My sister-in-law got empty pill capsules that we filled with little notes about things Mom had done for us that we were thankful for. She opened a capsule each day as she took her chemotherapy pills and the memories we shared meant the world to her. She loved her capsules and she loved us. It hurt her to move in bed because her bones were so sore, so we got her a thick feather bed to sleep on and it relieved some of her pain. It was a hard and emotionally draining time but a healing one, too. We were all able to tell Mom the things we needed to and we were together for strength and support.

 I was attending St. Thomas Parish and we had a tremendous priest who was full of love, acceptance and grace. His name was Father Bernard Keating and he had left his family in Ireland to serve God in the states. I brought him to my mother and he prayed over her. I watched her face go from tight, anxious and stricken to relaxed, peaceful and full of light. She accepted God's unconditional love for her and she was at peace. To watch her spiritual healing was a great gift to me.

 Mom suffered terribly at the end of her life but she was very brave and showed us all how to die with dignity and grace. I was so proud of her. She told us all that when she left, she would leave on a star. I thought that was a little strange but of course I didn't say anything to that effect. I just kept on loving her.

 I watched her take her last breath and when

another breath didn't follow it, I was devastated, empty, sad and angry. So much of her life had been wasted with unhappiness and bitterness. She could have been so happy if only her mental illness had been diagnosed and she had received help. Why had it taken so long for her to find God and then die so soon? Her life was over and we had all failed. I cried until my tears were gone and my head ached and throbbed.

My sister-in-law came screaming inside from the deck saying she saw a shooting star go across the sky. I couldn't take the drama so I went into the bedroom by myself and I talked to God. I told Him that I needed to know that my mom was OK. I told Him that I would go on with my life and be all right if I could just be sure that my mother was finally happy. I begged Him to give me some sort of sign to let me know that Mom was with Him and that I didn't need to worry about her any more. A few days later I got through Mom's celebration of life and then all my family left for their homes.

The next day I headed out on a run with my daughter Jennifer who was ten years old. We were living in a house on the side of a butte at that time. There were only about seven houses on our cinder road. We took off down the road and after about a quarter mile or so something came down out of the sky in front of us. It was an extremely bright, blinding light, with a multi-colored tail. I can hardly believe it myself but I can still see it clearly in my mind. It landed (or disappeared) about thirty feet in front of us. My daughter asked me what it was. I told her maybe fireworks??? (This was in February.)

She said, "Do you think that was Minah?" (My mom's name from the kids).

I was so glad that my daughter was with me because I was in shock. Of course, it was Minah. A shooting star that magnificent, with those colors in its tail, flying down off our butte and landing in the road before us, had to be Minah. I had asked for a sign and God had given me one that couldn't be mistaken. Shooting stars didn't come off the hill in the middle of the day right in front of us with brilliant light and colors in their tail, and then disappear before our eyes. Mom had said that she would leave on a star and I was skeptical. My sister-in-law had seen the star leave my parent's house and shoot across the sky right after she died and I had been skeptical. But I felt no skepticism about the star I had just seen, the star that God had sent to tell me my mom was with Him and happy after all. What Jennifer and I had just seen was an answer to sincere prayer that only God was capable of giving and He didn't stop there. No,

God always gives more than we ask because that is how He loves us.

That night while I was sleeping, my mother came to say goodbye. I felt her arms around me holding me in my bed and I smelled her perfume. I started sobbing in my sleep and my husband woke me up in concern. Mom left then and I could let her go because I knew without a doubt that she was alive and happy. You see, God knew the little girl who had suffered so many years with worry about her mother. He had been with me, felt my pain and He wanted me healed and at peace. I was scared when my mom was dying because of all the awful things that had happened in her life. I so wanted God to accept and love her.

I was only thirty-four and still had a lot to learn about God. He knew all about my mom's suffering with mental illness and all the hard things she had been through in her life and He never expected her to be perfect. His love is so much bigger than that. He wanted her to be happy even more than I did. He knew her and loved her even more than I did and He let me see that, because He knew and loved me, too.

God has continued the miracle and our glimpse into eternity. My mom has been allowed to show up twice that I know of in the last twenty years. I've felt her presence and talked to her often but twice we saw her again.

The first time was ten years later at a football game. Our son Tommy was a sophomore in high school and played half-back on the varsity football team. We were coming to the end of our last league game and needed a touchdown to win and go on to the state play-offs. It was fourth down, over ten yards to go and looked pretty hopeless. The center snapped the ball and Tommy ran his pattern from a slot position across the middle of the field. The quarterback threw the ball in his direction and Tommy went up for the catch. But he didn't come down. He hung in the air, suspended above the ground until the ball arrived and he reached back behind him to make the catch for the first down. As the chain crew reset the chains on the field and the players huddled up, guess what happened? A huge shooting star shot across the sky right over the stands on the opposite side of the field and disappeared. A murmur went through the crowd.

The announcer in the press box said in disbelief, "Did you all see that shooting star go over the stands on the other side of the field? I have never seen a shooting star so early in the evening or so low in the sky!"

My father, two of my siblings, some nieces and

nephews and all my children were sitting in a row in the grandstand and we all knew that Mom was there. I had goose bumps. Mom had been at that game and she had been allowed to hold Tommy up in the air until the football reached his hands. Then she said goodbye to all of us as she flew past and out of sight.

    I didn't see her the next time she came. It was four years later and my daughter Jennifer (who is named after my mother) was getting married. Jennifer was our first child to get married and I was so excited and happy. I missed my mom a lot and I knew how much she would have wanted to see Jennifer walking down the aisle. We had the rehearsal dinner at a park just outside of town. The guests stayed late and we ended up cleaning up in the dark. We all headed home and Jennifer and her best friend Karen brought up the rear. As they were driving down the dark road, a very big, bright shooting star went right across the windshield. They were so excited when they got home. My mother was there after all, sharing in the excitement of Jennifer's marriage, and God in His great love allowed us to know it.

    Through all of these experiences God proved His reality, His love and His caring about the things in life that are important to me. He let me peek into heaven and know that life is eternal and that His love is bigger than all of our poor and sinful choices. He taught me that we don't have to be perfect to deserve eternal life but that our love is what is important.

The apostle Paul shared with us in 1 Corinthians 13 that three gifts remain, faith, hope and love, but the greatest of these is love. Jesus gave us a new commandment, that we love one another. In spite of my mother's mental illness which sometimes caused havoc in our lives, she had love and she loved us. Love was enough.

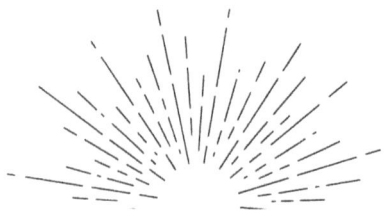

NINE

Forgiveness Times Four

"You find the strength to forgive when you recognize your own sin"

"Don't compare Julie and Molly until the first grade," the NICU doctor told me when I took the twins home from the hospital. "Julie has been sick and it will take her a long time to catch up with Molly."

I was fine with those words. Julie was alive and I was rejoicing.

However, Julie was weak in her muscle tone. I carried her everywhere with me, constantly talking to both babies. All the children helped entertain, so the twins had constant stimulation. An appointment was scheduled to check the twins with the doctor who had put the unsecured catheter in Julie in the NICU. My husband took time off work to accompany me. We were worried about

Julie. The doctor told us that Julie was perfect. I questioned him about her lack of strength and he repeated that she was "perfect". That's what we wanted to hear so we continued on caring for our girls and giving them every opportunity to grow and develop. Molly got bigger, filled out and started to move around. Julie got bigger, filled out, but stayed very floppy and couldn't move.

My parents were visiting us when Julie and Molly were eight months old. My mom and I went upstairs to get them out of their cribs after their nap. When we got to their room, I broke down and started sobbing. I told my mom that something was wrong with Julie and I didn't know what to do. In spite of what the doctors said in the NICU and at the babies' check-up, I couldn't ignore any longer that she wasn't developing. My mom held me and listened. We decided that I would make another appointment with my own pediatrician to ask questions about Julie.

I took Julie into the pediatrician and he checked her over. He said he wanted me to take her to a specialist and get another opinion. He made the appointment for me with a doctor who had been called in to see Julie in the NICU. I took Julie to that appointment with dread but also anxious to receive valid information. The doctor checked her over and said he would get back to me on the results of his exam. A month passed and I didn't hear anything. I saw the pediatrician for the twins' ear infections and asked him if I had given the specialist enough time to get back to me. The pediatrician became angry when he heard I still didn't have any answers and he told me that he would call the specialist.

That afternoon I got a phone call from the specialist. He told me Julie had cerebral palsy and tried to get off the phone immediately. I didn't know very much about cerebral palsy and I started asking questions. I asked him how she ended up with cerebral palsy when her APGAR scores (numbers they use to determine a baby's overall condition at birth) had been so high and she had seemed so healthy? He said her left kidney had hemorrhaged and clots had been sloughed out of the kidney and traveled through her body. He said the clots had lodged in her brain causing vessels to burst. In essence she had strokes at two days of age. He said the bleeds in her brain from the strokes had caused the cerebral palsy. I asked what had caused the kidney to hemorrhage and he said that had never been decided. I started asking about what Julie's future would hold. I asked if she would walk, if she would have learning disabilities or trouble with schoolwork, if she would grow and develop normally and how long it would take her to get stronger. He asked me why I wanted to know all these answers. I couldn't believe his attitude. He didn't want to talk to me and didn't think I should be asking questions.

I said, "If Julie was your daughter would you want to know the answers to my questions?"

He said that he guessed I had a point. I asked what we could do for Julie to help her now. He said I should start physical therapy with Julie and he would call the PT department at the hospital and give a referral.

After talking with the specialist and getting a diagnosis I started investigating what had happened to Julie in the hospital. I went to the hospital Records department and asked to see Julie's file. The receptionist told me I would have to make an appointment. I told her I was entitled to Julie's records without an appointment and I wanted to see her records. She left me at the desk and was gone a long time. When she returned, she told me Julie's records weren't there. I asked which doctor had them checked out. She said no one had them checked out; they just couldn't find them. I knew she was lying but I didn't know what to do. She said a hospital release form was found in Julie's chart and I could see that. I took a copy home. Julie's release records said she had suffered a brain insult, probably from encephalitis. Julie had never had encephalitis in the nursery. It had never even been mentioned! The whole discharge was a lie.

 My sister had a good friend who worked in a NICU in another hospital. I talked to her and told her about Julie's birth history, the unsecured catheter, kidney failure and seizure. She said one possible side effect of an umbilical artery catheter being done incorrectly was kidney or heart damage. Those three arteries are connected. She said the doctor could have hit the renal artery when placing the catheter. Even more likely, it could have slipped into the renal artery because it was left unsecured and when Julie was given an antibiotic through the catheter it could have gone directly into the kidney and caused it to hemorrhage. She said they should have told me in the hospital what happened to Julie and it sounded like they were covering up the doctor's mistake.

 I eventually got a copy of Julie's hospital chart and it did state that Julie's catheter had been left unsecured and that her kidney was discovered to have hemorrhaged when the neonatologist came on duty the next morning. The nurse's notes about the catheter insertion and discovered kidney hemorrhage stopped mid-sentence and were missing from the chart for that shift. Both of the X-rays that were done to look at Julie's kidney stated *imaging insufficient to see the cause of renal failure*. What are the chances that both X-rays had insufficient imaging? The hospital system was careful to put no evidence of wrongdoing in Julie's chart.

It took three precious months to get Julie scheduled into physical therapy at the hospital. When we did start therapy, the PT taught me ways to position Julie that would help her to get stronger and things to do at home to strengthen her. She played movement games with Julie and Julie initiated the games back to her. The PT was thrilled because she could tell that Julie was smart. She gave me a book to read on how to help a child with cerebral palsy. I read the book from cover to cover before our next appointment and I felt like someone had stabbed my heart with a knife. The book stressed the importance of the first year of life in a child who has cerebral palsy. It told all the things a family could do to help their child develop and gain strength. We had spent our first year being told not to compare Julie to Molly, being told she was perfect and waiting for calls from doctors and appointments to get help for her. Now we had missed the first critical year of her care. I was so very angry. Not only had the NICU doctors hurt Julie, but even worse they had not allowed us to help her because they were trying to cover up what they had done. She should have been having therapy that entire first year when her brain was growing. They had hurt her twice! To make matters worse, they didn't provide long-term therapy for children. The physical therapist saw Julie for two months and then told me that she was getting pressure to pass Julie on to Shriner's Hospital. So now they were hurting Julie for the third time. First, they hemorrhaged her kidney, second, they didn't tell us what was wrong with her so we could help her, and third they wouldn't provide the care she needed after they hurt her. I was a kind and trustful person and I couldn't come to terms with what had happened to my baby. I became angry and depressed.

    I had six young children to care for and almost no time to grieve for my baby. I was able to get through each day with the children but would shut down around my husband. I couldn't find the grace inside me to forgive the NICU doctor for what he had done to my baby. I prayed and realized that a mistake had been made with the catheter, but not made on purpose. The lies they told me and the lack of care for Julie and our family was on purpose and that was harder for me to accept. They cared more about covering up a mistake and protecting a doctor than they did about a new, innocent, precious baby. My husband got frustrated with my depression and told me I had to get over it. I found a Christian counselor through a church and made an appointment.

During my visit I asked her, "How do you forgive someone who has hurt your baby, left her disabled for life and then lied to you about it?"

Her reply will stay with me for the rest of my life.

She told me, "You find the strength to forgive when you recognize your own sin."

I went back to God on my knees and begged Him to help me. I asked Him to show me my sin in all its fullness and my sin rose before my eyes. I had done so many hurtful things over my lifetime. That doctor's sin of arrogance and pride was no worse than many of mine. I told God that I wanted to be able to forgive that doctor. I wanted to forgive because He in His wisdom required forgiveness of me but that doctor had hurt my baby so terribly that I absolutely couldn't forgive him. God spoke to me in the silence that followed. He told me that Jesus could forgive him for me. Jesus would stand with me at the throne and do the forgiving. He would do for me what I could not do for myself. I felt relief in my spirit for the first time in weeks. I pictured Jesus with me in the presence of God.

Jesus said, "Father, I stand in Linda's place and I forgive the doctor for hurting Julie."

I was flooded with peace and started to enjoy my life again. I found a big brother in Jesus who could do for me the very thing I couldn't do for myself. I found one more reason to love Jesus.

The second year of the twins' life brought another heartache to work through. I had always wanted to have twins but I had pictured something different. I had pictured two identical girls dressing alike and playing together, trading places and confusing people; kind of like the movie, *Parent Trap*, I had watched as a little girl. My little girls were identical but one of them had weak muscle tone so she looked a little different. Only when they were crying or sleeping did they look totally identical. More devastating, however, was the fact that one toddler was learning to sit, stand and walk and the other one wasn't. I asked God what kind of sick joke this was to give me Julie with cerebral palsy and Molly developing so perfectly so that I could never escape from what Julie couldn't do. After a few weeks of being angry at God over the difference in the girls, I started realizing that Molly was the best gift that Julie could have. I had an identical child to watch and show me what Julie should be doing at each age. By helping Julie to do the same normal activities that Molly was doing, like opening kitchen drawers and emptying them, Julie was able to keep up cognitively and learn appropriate things. Julie and Molly always had a friend to play with and they played brilliantly.

 I got angry at God a lot that year. I told Him all kinds of things I didn't like about what He had allowed. I told Him that I hated him. A few years earlier when I was really growing in my love of God and Jesus, I had prayed a deep soul prayer. I had asked God to make me like Jesus. I was all in and totally committed to being His daughter, to be used for His purposes. I wanted to love like Jesus, think like Jesus and be transformed into a child like Him. I told God at that time that I could give Him everything in my life, but please, just please don't let anything happen to my children. I couldn't totally release my children because I loved them so desperately. I was a young Christian and a young mother. If I had possessed more wisdom, I would have thrown my children in His direction. I would have understood that He loved them even more than I did and that I couldn't protect them from everything this world could do to them. I couldn't protect Julie from a doctor's negligence because

God gave that doctor a free will.

It turned out that the doctor had been taking extra shifts at the hospital to make more money. He was later sued for malpractice by his second wife for one million dollars. He was prideful and arrogant. God didn't intervene to stop him from hurting Julie and I was angry because I thought He should have. Hadn't I trusted Him for all of my life? Shouldn't that be enough to protect me and mine from the free will of others? In my immaturity, I was trying to play God and make up His rules. He never promised me that my life or the lives of my family would be easy and pain free. He only promised to stay with me, love me and tum to good the evil that was allowed to happen. He did save Julie's life when we gave her back to Him in the NICU nursery and trusted her to Him. I had to trust that He would tum this doctor's prideful choice in doing a procedure he shouldn't have done into something good and beautiful.

After Julie was diagnosed with cerebral palsy she went through a battery of tests. We were told many different and sometimes contradictory predictions about Julie's future, but one specialist said that Julie would probably walk at two years of age. That was one prediction I held onto hard and fast. Eventually, Julie and Molly's second birthday rolled around. Molly was walking and running like every other two-year-old, but Julie still needed pillows surrounding her when she sat on the floor in case she fell over. She was still pretty weak even after all the physical and occupational therapy we were getting for her.

When the twins went down for their nap on that second birthday, I put Molly in her crib first and then I rocked Julie. I decided to take a nap also, so I put Julie in bed with me and held her close. The enormity of the fact that it was her second birthday and she was still not even close to walking enveloped me. I started to blame God again and ask my why questions. Why could You let this happen when I loved You? Why did that doctor have to be on duty when my babies were born? Why does Julie have to suffer her entire life for a doctor's mistake? I began to sob and sob from deep in my spirit. Then something happened. I felt a shocking warmth and heat enter into my core. I felt, *literally felt*, arms enfold me and hold me. And I heard as plainly as if they were spoken, the words, *I love you*. A huge peace enveloped me and I lay there in His holy love. God didn't answer any of my questions, or did He? Did I hear *I love you* as an answer to my questions or as a comfort to his beloved child? Did He allow Julie to get hurt for some greater good for me? It was too much to fathom so I lay there for a long time soaking in His love. He told me He loves me and whatever His answer meant, I knew that I could trust Him with my life and the life of my daughter. God was big enough for my pain and He would be big enough for Julie's as well.

My encounter with God on Julie and Molly's second birthday helped me progress further with my forgiveness battle. Forgiveness had never been my strong suit. Recognizing my own sin, Jesus standing with me at the throne of God and God holding and loving me on that second birthday were huge stepping stones toward my healing and being able to truly forgive what I had thought was unforgiveable. But the forgiveness wasn't yet complete and the way it would be completed I never saw coming.

Every night when we put our children to bed my husband and I would pray with them. After I put the twins down for the night, I would often sing songs that they liked and then listen to each of them pray. One of these nights when they were three, I was sitting between their beds. I had sung their songs and listened to each of their prayers. Julie prayed last and she thanked God for all of her family and the horses and cows and trees. We lived in a rural area with lots of animals in the fields and she was already an animal lover. I kissed each of the girls, told them that God loved them and started to leave the room.

Julie spoke up saying, "Mommy, I don't think God loves me." I was startled by her statement.

"Why do you say that Julie, of course God loves you very much," I answered.

"If God loved me, He would have made me like Molly," she said.

Oh my God! No Julie. Don't think that, I screamed inside.

"Julie, God did make you like Molly. He made you exactly like Molly, sweetheart. When you were born, you were strong and held your head up in the delivery room. You were stronger than Molly. Julie, a doctor made a mistake when you were in the hospital. He made a mistake and hurt you and caused you to have cerebral palsy. He didn't mean to hurt you. He didn't do it on purpose and he felt really bad after it happened. But God didn't hurt you, honey. It was the doctor's fault. God loves you Julie and He saved your life after the doctor hurt you. Do you understand? Do you understand that God made you like Molly but a doctor hurt you by accident?" I asked.

"Yes," she whispered.

"I'm glad you understand sweetheart. Never think that God doesn't love you. He loved you enough to want you to live when you got hurt."

I kissed both girls again. Then Julie spoke the words that changed me forever.

"Mommy, Let's pray for the doctor."

I went numb inside, but I got back down on my knees and I prayed with Julie for that doctor who had hurt her.

I said, "Father, Julie, Molly and I lift up the doctor from the NICU who hurt Julie. We know he didn't mean to Father and we ask that you forgive him for what he did and that You bless him. Amen."

I left their room and when I closed the door, I collapsed against the wall with tears streaming down my face. I had prayed for that doctor who I had hated for three years. I prayed for him at my three-year old daughter's request. The child he had hurt had forgiven him and prayed for him. I could do no less. My forgiveness was complete and God had accomplished it through the very victim of the doctor's sin, my precious, precious, daughter.

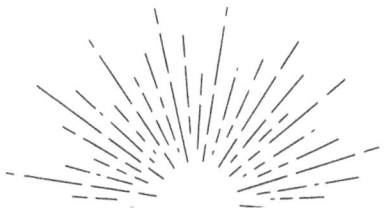

TEN

Covered With Prayer

There are no "what ifs" in God's world.

It was just after New Years when the dreams began. I couldn't get a handle on them at first. I would wake up in the middle of the night in a sweat, or in the morning with a sense of fear and dread, but I wasn't sure why. I would go over in my mind where each of our six children was, and I began calling them to check in more often, but the dreams continued. Finally, one night the dream was so vivid that I saw my husband's face and realized that it was he who was dying in my dream. I was shaken. For a few days I studied him closely. I didn't say anything at first because I have been accused a time or two of overreacting and worrying too much, but I saw that my husband's coloring had changed. He looked tired and kind of gray. I told myself that it was

February in Oregon, he obviously hadn't been in the sun for a while, and it made sense his coloring would be paler. It was the grayish tinge, though, that really bothered me. I started asking him how he felt, if he was overly tired, if he was sleeping well. Every time I looked at him my heart jumped a little because his color reminded me of my mother's coloring when she was dying of breast cancer.

I finally told Jerry what I was thinking. He was surprised and told me he was fine. His back was flaring up with his arthritis (he thought) and it kept him from sleeping well. He said he probably looked white and tired from the pain. I told him about my dreams that were continuing and made him promise to call for a physical appointment with our family doctor. He called, and the first appointment for a well patient physical was in May. It seemed an eternity away, but I tried not to worry. At least he had a scheduled appointment.

During that spring, we made a few trips over the mountain to Portland. It seemed like we were hitting every rest stop on the way and I told Jerry that we needed to drink less coffee. The pain in his low back was getting increasingly worse as well. The pain showed in his face but he didn't complain or take his discomfort out on any of us.

He just kept his happy disposition and a smile on his graying face.

May finally came around and Jerry had his physical. He came home upbeat. The doctor hadn't found anything wrong but was running blood tests and would call with the results. He called a week later and every score was within normal range except cholesterol. Medicine was ordered to help lower that. That doctor told my husband that one test he had ordered hadn't been run by the lab. It was a PSA test to check for prostate cancer risk. The doctor said that the test was only run for men over fifty and my husband was only forty-four so they skipped it. He said he would reorder the test if Jerry wanted it, but there were no signs of anything wrong to warrant the test. Jerry hesitated. He had recently read an article about PSA tests and how important they were. He said to reorder the test.

The day Jerry went into the lab to get the blood draw, the lab was crowded with people waiting. He had a list of errands to do for the house he was building and couldn't wait. He decided not to get the test after all and turned to leave. Our doctor's nurse just happened to be walking by the lab and stopped to greet Jerry. Jerry told her he was going to forgo the PSA test because he couldn't wait. She took him into a room and did the blood draw herself. When his PSA score came back a few days later it was an eight and anything over a four was bad news. An appointment was scheduled with Dr. O'Hollaren, a urologist who happened to be our neighbor. Jerry saw him in July. Dr. O'Hollaren felt a growth in the prostate right away and did a biopsy to send away to the lab. The results would take a couple weeks to get back.

Our fourth child, Tommy was entering his senior year of high school. It was summer, and we had scheduled a vacation for the entire family before he graduated. Jerry didn't want to cancel our trip so we headed for Hawaii the day before the test results were due. When we landed on Oahu and were waiting for our connection to Maui, Jerry called for the test results. He had cancer and they wanted to see him immediately. He scheduled an appointment for the day after we were to arrive home.

Our time in Hawaii was bittersweet. We told the children about their dad's cancer and we all prayed over him. They all adore him and were concerned, but we all went into denial and joked about it and became very determined to have fun and create memories. Jerry and I went to a bookstore and starting reading about prostate cancer and how to cure it naturally. Again, we were in denial. We did find out the warning signs of prostate cancer. Jerry had only two of them: more frequent urination and low back ache. That explained the stops on our trips over the mountains and the worsening pain in his back.

I had never heard of the prostate before this time. I grew up in the fifties and sixties and barely knew my reproductive parts let alone the male ones! We learned that surgery on the prostate could very possibly cause impotency in men. It could also cause urinary control problems. If the cancer reached the lymph nodes in the groin area, death was certain. It was all very disturbing and we were both in shock. We covered it all with laughter and fun during the day for the children and clung to each other at night.

The day after we returned to our home we were at the urologist's office. The nurse called Jerry back and the doctor came out and talked to me alone. He explained to me the options Jerry had: watch and wait, radiation therapy, and a radical prostatectomy or removal of the prostate. He said that during the surgery the first priority was to save life, the second was to save continence and the third was to save potency. I told him Jerry had been my best friend since I was sixteen, we had six children, we were only forty-four and I just wanted him alive. He also warned me Jerry would suffer depression after the surgery. I told him Jerry was the most positive person I had ever known and he probably wouldn't get depressed. He said everyone got depressed after the surgery.

When the doctor went over our options with both of us together, he told us watch and wait wasn't a good idea for someone in their forties. Radiation would probably only give us seven years before recurrence and then we could not do surgery. He said the only safe option was surgery and he would do everything possible to save continence and potency. My husband asked how long the recovery would be after surgery and I instantly knew what his concern was. Football daily doubles started the next Monday and our son was a senior who started both ways on the team and loved football. Jerry was the head coach and the team had a chance to take state. The doctor said Jerry would be down about a week and have a catheter for two weeks. After that it depended on the person but most stayed out of work at least a month. I told the doctor my husband was thinking about football and wanting to put the surgery off until November. The biopsy had only found cancer in four of the twelve prostate samples and November wasn't totally out of the question but it was taking a chance. I said we either have to do the surgery tomorrow or wait until November.

The doctor said, "Let's do it tomorrow."

We actually did it two days later because we needed a day for Jerry to do the fasting and cleansing to prepare for the surgery.

The next day, we took our son Tommy to visit football coaches at University of Oregon and Oregon State. Jerry took huge bottles of horrid tasting solution that he had to drink throughout the day to prepare for surgery. By midday I was starving so I ordered two sandwiches for Tommy and me. I handed Tommy a sandwich but he said he wasn't hungry.

I said, "What?"

I had spent the last four years feeding that kid huge amounts of food to help him keep weight on for football. He was still trying to gain weight and he was refusing food? I wanted an explanation and "I'm not hungry," wasn't cutting it so I demanded an honest answer.

"Are you sick? Are you worried about Dad? What am I going to do with this sandwich? What's wrong with you?"

Finally, in desperation and under his breath Tommy said, "Mom, I'm fasting."

I was stunned.

"What did you say?" I asked to his frustration. "I'm fasting for Dad," he said quietly.

Fast and pray, fast and pray; that's when I knew just how much Jerry's cancer was affecting this son who looked so much like him, acted like him and loved him beyond measure. It occurred to me then that our children, just like me, were faking normalcy during the day while they bargained with God on the side.

As Jerry was checking into the hospital the following morning, we looked up and Uncle Woelfle, my husband's best friend from high school, was standing there. He had heard through the grapevine about the cancer and had driven over the mountain to be there for us. My husband, all six foot four, two hundred forty pounds of him started to cry. He had remained strong for me but could let down his guard with his best friend. I will be forever grateful for that dear friend's show of love and kindness.

The surgery plan was to first test Jerry's lymph nodes and make sure there was no cancer in them. If there was cancer they would stop the surgery, close him up and have Jerry get his things in order before he died. Dr. O'Hollaren was going to let me know when the lymph nodes were clear and then the surgery would continue. I waited and waited with our dear friend. The time we should have heard about the lymph nodes came and went and we kept waiting. I got increasingly agitated and found it hard to keep praying. Fear was taking hold. Finally, we received word that the lymph nodes were clear and the surgery would continue.

The next day we found out why the wait during surgery had been so long. Dr. O'Hollaren came into our room and sat down to talk. The biopsy on Jerry's prostate had been deceiving. When they got inside his abdomen during surgery, they found cancer throughout the prostate and covering the nerves all the way to the lymph nodes. The lymph nodes were sent to the lab and the results came back negative, but Dr. O'Hollaren took off for the lab to check them out himself before continuing on with the surgery. After seeing how much cancer was in Jerry and how far it had spread, he couldn't believe there was no cancer in the lymph nodes, but none was to be found. He also told us the cancer had left the prostate and grown arms out into the abdominal cavity. The surgery had been extensive and gone on until all margins of tissue were clear. We were both in shock and felt sick to our stomachs.

Jerry had been so close to death. He was going to need radiation to kill any possible cancer cells that might remain and Dr. O'Hollaren didn't want to wait the usual month to start it. He recommended radiation be started after two weeks, even though Jerry wouldn't be healed from the surgery. He said it would be very hard on Jerry but would give him the best chance to live.

The only complaining my dear husband did during the whole ordeal was when he couldn't eat for five days. He kept trying, with no success, to talk the doctor into letting him eat. In fact, he whined so much about being hungry that it got embarrassing! Dr. O'Hollaren wouldn't take any chances of complications after that extensive surgery and he held his ground on no food. Finally, the days passed and the OK for food was received. That evening there was a knock on the hospital room door. I opened it and there stood a server from the best steak restaurant in town. She had two complete full course steak dinners with a bottle of amazing red wine and dessert. She set it up in our room, compliments of Dr.O'Hollaren. That was such a sweet gift for us from an amazing man who had already given us my husband's life. We will be eternally grateful.

Jerry came home from the hospital with two weeks left on a catheter. He missed the first week of football practice, but sent practice plans for his assistants to carry out. He arrived for practice the second week with a catheter strapped to his leg and a golf cart to get around the field. He started radiation after two weeks and went every morning before school to be radiated. He never missed a day of practice or school. He rarely complained about how the radiation burned him and he never got depressed.

It has been twenty-five years since Jerry's surgery. He has worked to put our children through college, seen them get married, met thirteen grandchildren and two service dogs. He has had special vacation time with me and grown ever closer to his God. I think back on his cancer experience and wonder, *What if?* *What if I hadn't listened to the warnings in my dreams? What if he hadn't chosen to repeat the PSA test? What if the nurse hadn't happened by when he was leaving the lab without doing the test? What if Tommy hadn't fasted and prayed? What if we all hadn't prayed? What if the doctor hadn't opened a spot for surgery so soon and Jerry had waited until football was over? What if the surgeon hadn't done such an extensive surgery? What if he hadn't started radiation so soon?*

There are no 'what ifs' in God's world. We go through our lives and we have free will to make decisions. We listen to God's voice or we don't. There have been times that we didn't, with drastic consequences. This time we did. We choose to ask for God's help in prayer or we don't. This time we did. We choose to care about and serve others or we are too busy. This time the nurse chose to care. We choose great surgeons or we don't. This time we did. So many places we could have gone wrong and we didn't. We chose to seek God and to trust and pray. We let Him do His work and he saved us.

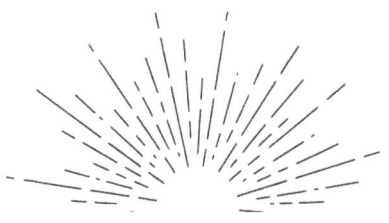

ELEVEN

In His Time or Never Give Up

*Pray without ceasing and trust
Him with your whole heart.*

Dad walked through the back door and into my kitchen. He looked different: happier, calm, peaceful. I was forty-eight and he was seventy-five. I hadn't seen him very much since my mom died, fifteen years before. He became busy with his new life and his new wife. We didn't have much in common anymore. He said he had something to tell me and he sat down on a bar stool and started to talk. I had waited forty-five years to hear what he had to say, but let me back up to the beginning.

Because I loved God at a very young age, I prayed every night and tried to please God in my daily life. Over the years, I realized that my father didn't understand my faith. We didn't talk about faith but he wasn't keen to go to church or helpful in getting us there. My mom took us to church, mostly on holidays. I overheard conversations where my father would share how "religious" my grandmother was and how he hated being made to go to church every Sunday. I loved my grandmother even though I rarely saw her. I always felt a closeness with her, like we were kindred spirits.

When I was in high school, I attended Young Life with my friends. We sang Christian songs and heard teachings and testimonies from college leaders. My girlfriends and I attended Bible study and read the New Testament. I learned so much about Jesus's life. God became my center, the first love in my life. I began asking my father about his faith. We had deep and sometimes heated discussions about Christianity and about how close God could really be in a person's life; about how close He was to me in my life. Dad kind of humored me at first and made light of my zealous faith. Eventually, as I cornered him about the reality of a living, personally involved God, he shared his real feelings with me. He told me he believed there might be a supreme being or God controlling the universe somewhere. To even begin to accept that "God" would be personal or know or care about him as an individual was something he had never been able to consider. It just didn't make any sense to him. It wasn't rational or even remotely possible in his mind. I prayed to God that He would show my dad just how personal and caring He really was.

Over the years I had learned things about my dad that helped me understand why he might not think he could believe in a personal God who cared about him as an individual. Dad was the fourth of six children in his family. When he was two years old his nine-year-old brother Dale was diagnosed with leukemia. Dale and my grandfather were very close because Dale was the oldest boy in the family. As he got sicker and weaker, Dale would beg my grandfather to please not let him die. But he did die and my grandparents were devastated. Grandpa shut down and cried all the time. Grandma had to keep going with a broken heart while she cared for 11-year-old Beryl, 5-year-old Carol, and 2-year-old Glen (my dad). A few months later Carol got sick and was diagnosed with the same leukemia that had killed Dale. Carol died within the next year. That was the first recorded time in history that two children in the same family had ever died of that kind of leukemia. This left Beryl and my dad (now ages 12 and 3) as the only surviving children. I can only imagine what Dad's preschool years were like. He was being raised by grieving parents who couldn't have been too attentive and his first impressions of his world were of extreme grief and despair.

Dad was extremely athletic. He played every sport that was offered at his school and he was a star in each one. He especially loved basketball and would spend every minute he could bouncing a ball. He was forbidden to stay after school to play each day, but he stayed anyway. He would rather suffer the woodshed sessions with the belt than miss any time playing sports. Grandma always said that Dad would do the very thing he wanted regardless of the consequences. She was mostly right, but one story I had heard gave me hope for him to change. When Dad refused to come home after school, Grandpa was forced to discipline him in the woodshed. This went on day after day, week after week. Then one day after the whipping with Grandpa's belt, Dad looked up and saw tears running down Grandpa's cheeks. Dad said that those tears finally made him want to come home after school. My dad did have a heart inside his stubborn and somewhat self-centered exterior. He was able to love someone more than himself.

Dad was so talented in athletics that he had to pick a sport to play in college and he picked basketball. He got a full ride basketball scholarship to Oregon State and he was the only member of his family to ever graduate from college. My father had all the worldly gifts he needed. He was very handsome and popular with the girls. He excelled at all sports and started at forward for the Oregon State Beavers throughout college. He was very bright and was at the top of his classes when he decided to apply himself. He graduated with a teaching degree in English and Physical Education. He became a basketball coach and he was very successful at it.

I was always proud of my dad growing up. He got the most out of the talent he had on his basketball squads and always beat teams that were bigger, stronger and faster. He treated his players with respect and cared very much about them as people. He came up with new offenses and defenses and was sought after to speak at many coaching clinics. He taught at clinics with John Wooden from UCLA and they became friends. Dad had the first undefeated team in the state of Oregon in 1970 when I was a sophomore in high school. I was so happy for him when his team claimed their state championship trophy. He won over seven hundred games in his career and he coached until he was seventy-five years old, but he had another life going on during those years as well.

Dad had trouble being faithful in his marriage. He lived a life sprinkled with lies. I don't know why he was unfaithful. Maybe he needed to rebel like he had growing up. Maybe he didn't want anyone telling him what to do or trying to control him in any way. Maybe it was my mom's mental illness that he didn't know how to live with. As the years went by my mom became more and more difficult. Looking at the two of them it was hard to tell who had caused whom to become what they became. Did my dad's cheating set off my mom's illness? I do know that by hiding the sin in his life throughout those years, and ignoring the way that sin hurt others, Dad made it harder on himself to come to know God. He finally got tired of the lying and the pain it caused, and he made a vow to never lie again. I am convinced that was the beginning of his heart's preparation to receive God into his life.

After Mom died of breast cancer when she was fifty-seven, Dad disappeared from my life. Two days after Mom died, the cancer support lady who had visited Mom when she was dying called my dad and invited him to dinner. The day we spread our mother's ashes he couldn't stay and have dinner with all of us because he had to go to a political rally with her. He married her after only seven months and she was very controlling and wanted nothing to do with his family. It was all about her and her kids and Dad went along. It was very hurtful to us. I felt like I had lost my mother and father, and eventually as the years past I forgot to even think of him when family holidays or events took place. He kind of disappeared.

Eventually his marriage didn't work out and he started to resurface again.

Now he was sitting in my kitchen and he wanted to tell me something that seemed very important to him. I knew he was dating someone new. She had been a friend of my mom's and I liked her. He told me that they had just returned from eastern Oregon where she owned a hotel. They had gone over to do some repairs on the building and he had climbed high on a ladder to paint. He had slipped on the ladder and twisted his back so badly that he couldn't stand up straight or walk. He had lain in bed for a few days. When he finally got up and tried to walk bent over, a guest at the motel asked him what had happened. Dad told him, and the guest asked Dad if he would let him lay hands on his back and pray for healing.

Dad said, "Sure."

The man sat Dad down on a chair, laid his

hands on my dad's back and prayed for God to heal Dad's back in the Name of Jesus and by the power of the Holy Spirit. Dad said he felt heat and electricity run through his back and he shook on the chair. When he stood up his pain was almost gone and it disappeared over the next day. The man who prayed was very humble and thanked God for His healing power and love for my dad. I got chills all over when Dad told me about his healing. I was so excited God had shown him that He was personal to Dad as an individual, He cared about Dad's back and He wanted it healed. My father had experienced God in a very personal way, the way I had prayed he would.

But Dad wasn't done talking. There was more. As Dad was returning to his home from eastern Oregon, he fell asleep at the wheel of his car. He awoke just in time to see that he had crossed the center line and was traveling head on into a pickup truck. He told me his first reaction was to swerve off the road so he wouldn't hurt anyone. He sped off the road, over a ditch, flipped over down an embankment and smashed into a tree. As he hung upside down in his car in shock, the two men from the pickup truck made their way down the embankment to see who was dead. The car was completely smashed like an accordion, the top was caved in and the windows broken, but they found my father alive and he crawled out of the car and walked away with no injuries. The two men just happened to be pastors from a church in town and they had been heading off on a hunting expedition. The first thing they said to my father when he crawled out of the car was,

"Do you know God? because He sure loves you and He just saved your life."

They stayed and talked with my father until a tow truck came to take him back to town.

I was smiling so hard my face hurt, but there were tears in my eyes. Tears of joy were surfacing for the infinite love God had for my father, a love so deep that He found two miraculous ways to gain my father's attention. He let Dad know he was very special to Him and He wanted my dad to know Him personally. Even my father couldn't dispute that God had healed his back and saved his life. God had answered my prayers for my dad from so long ago and I'm sure my grandmother's prayers for her son were answered, too. God had also given me my father back. We began spending time together and I became closer than ever to him. God allowed us to repair the years we were apart and grow into the father and daughter we were meant to be.

Over the next fifteen years, Dad was able to enjoy his grandchildren and great-grandchildren.

He spent some holidays with us and attended weddings and graduations. Eventually, he showed signs of cognitive decline and was diagnosed with Alzheimer's disease. He lived close to us and I loved him. My oldest sister and I sat with him as he took his last breath. In my grief, I knew Dad had been redeemed. He had found his Savior and was going to meet Him face to face.

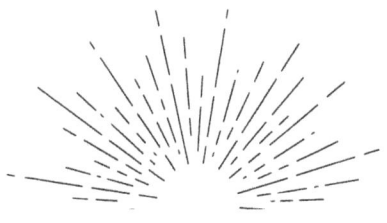

TWELVE

Only One Tail Light

When struggling with a child, pray, cling to God and trust Him for the ending.

Following two sisters, our third child was a boy. We named him Joseph which means increasing faithfulness. We named him after Joseph, son of Jacob, in the Old Testament. I had just studied Genesis in the Bible and Joseph's story touched my heart in a mighty way. Joseph knew extreme adversity, pain and betrayal but he never let his faith in God waiver. Joseph was his father's favorite child and he was sold into slavery by his jealous brothers. He ended up in Egypt as a slave in Potiphar's household. He repeatedly refused to sleep with Potiphar's wife when she tried to seduce him. For his faithfulness to God, she had him thrown into prison. He found favor with the prison guards and through his faith and trust in God, he eventually became Pharoah's trusted servant. Pharoah put him in charge of all of Egypt. God used Joseph to save his family during five years of famine.

Joseph's faith in God was so complete that he wasn't bitter and he didn't hold grudges against his brothers when they arrived in Egypt thinking he was dead. In Genesis chapter 50, verse 19-21 he says to his brothers:

> *"Don't be afraid. Am I in the place of God? You intended to harm me, but God intended it for good to accomplish what is now being done, the saving of many lives. So then, don't be afraid. I will provide for you and your children."*

Joseph didn't question the circumstances of his life but put all his trust in God and God was able to use his faith in a mighty way. That was the kind of faith I wanted for my baby boy, so we named him Joseph.

Our Joseph was unique from the start. He was amazingly content and loving. He slept with us at night and he would sleep until 11am as long as I was in bed snuggling him. He loved to be held, rocked and sung to. It seemed as if I rocked around the world and back that first year of his life while he snuggled me and his sisters played in the living room around us. He was the sweetest baby I had ever known, and his sweetness continued as he grew. When we would get together with other families and another child would take a toy away from Joey, he would stop and look at me as if to say, "I don't understand." Then he would go and get another toy and start to play again. I watched a child hit him with a bat when he was three and he looked at them confused and walked away. He said the sweetest things to everyone and was filled with love. My husband and I used to say that he was an angel here on earth because he was so amazingly loving and kind. I adored him so much that I told my husband we needed to have another baby or I would ruin Joseph.

As much as I loved the story of Joseph's faith in the Bible, I didn't take enough notice of Jacob's favoritism and how it affected Joseph's brothers. I loved all my children with all my heart but Joey was so sweet and kind that his sisters became jealous of him. We had lots of endearing nicknames for each other in our family and the girls started calling Joey, Jehosaphat. It was a Bible name and I thought it was cute. I had no idea what was really going on behind that name. Joey had stocky little legs and more baby fat than his sisters and they knew exactly what they were doing; "Joe's so fat". I didn't figure out what was going on until Joey was in the fourth grade and damage had been done. He thought he was fat and his self-image was affected. I immediately called a family meeting. We rarely had family meetings, but when we did the children (who were now 13, 11, 9, 7, 3 and 3) knew we meant business. The girls apologized to their brother for the unkind nickname they had saddled him with and my husband told all the children that he had been built just like Joey when he was young. The girls truly felt bad for the pain they had caused their brother and I never heard the name Jehosaphat mentioned again.

Joey's sweetness and kind heart did not serve him well as a boy in this world. Just as Joseph in the Bible was imprisoned for doing right, our Joey was being rejected for doing right. He never did understand how to fit in with the majority of boys who made fun of others to be cool. He was extremely bright in school, always at the top of every class. When he was in the fifth-grade, he changed his name to Joe and went out for football. Boys were divided into teams by weight and size. Joe was big for his age and ended up on a team with seventh graders. There is a huge difference in physical and emotional development between fifth and seventh grade boys not to mention that the seventh graders were in junior high as opposed to grade school. Joe wanted to play football like his dad and to fit in on his team. The coaches put him on the offensive line because he was big and inexperienced. Joe never complained but he seemed quieter and ever more insecure at home. I noticed large, ugly bruises on the top of his feet and asked where they came from. It turned out that in football practice one of the seventh graders would entertain himself and others by grinding his cleats into Joey's feet across the scrimmage line. I was furious, but Joe begged me to stay out of it. He made it through that year and three years later he was a sophomore in high school. By that time, he had matured and was a starter on his team. He played ahead of the kid who had ground bruises into his feet. True to himself, Joe was only kind to him.

I wish I could say that Joe, like Joseph in the Bible never changed his behavior but I can't. The world got to him and he became tired of being lonely and trying to fit in. He had always been the kid who helped everyone else in class and the teachers would sit him by a problem student because he was always kind and a good example.

In the sixth grade he began to act out in class to get attention. He made his classmates laugh and he made his teacher crazy. I talked to Joe and told him that I was going to go in and talk to his teacher. Joe got tears in his eyes and begged me not to go.

I'll never forget what he told me, "Please don't go in Mom. I finally got rid of my good guy image and I have friends."

He was acting out in a premeditated manner; a way he had figured out would help him survive in the environment he had to be in. I understood and I felt helpless to stop what was happening.

Joe went from bad to worse. He so enjoyed his newfound attention that he became ever more of a pain for his teachers. He purposely blew off his homework and tried to get bad grades. His baby fat was gone and he was a gorgeous guy and the girls took notice. He became friends with a group of popular kids who were experimenting with alcohol and marijuana. I tried to intervene. I went to junior high and sat in on his classes only to find classrooms out of control and incompetent teachers. I followed Joe after school and took him out of parties at parentless homes where the kids were smoking marijuana.

During his eighth-grade year, I told him if he got into trouble one more time, he would be coming home. The very next day I got a call from the school. Joe was in trouble. He had made his choice. I took him out of school all together and home schooled him. We had a wonderful time together. He worked hard for me, read classic literature and wrote amazing papers. I asked him why he did such great work for me when he had written barely a paragraph for assignments at school. He said if he gave me that terrible work, I would make him do it over. He had been living up to the very low expectations of his teachers. We worked out together each day for P.E. class and Joe began lifting weights. He got taller, bigger, and stronger that year. He was happy.

Joe went back to public school for high school. He was successful academically and in sports. He joined a youth group and seemed happy for a while but then he moved away from his new Christian friends. He thought they were judgmental. He started hanging out with truly nice guys but they all made bad choices and the drinking and drugs started up again. Joe did well academically and became captain of his football team and all league as a lineman, but he wasn't happy underneath it all. He was still trying to be "bad" to fit in and he wasn't being true to himself. I had no control over my seventeen-year-old son and had to trust God to watch over him.

Joe was arrested for theft his first month of college. He had played a prank with some fraternity brothers on another fraternity. They took all of the CDs from a party and ran off with them. We hired an attorney and went to court with him. He got a misdemeanor that was later expunged. He paid the attorney fees.

Joe changed schools a couple of times while working on an engineering degree. He always had a girlfriend and he always had a job. He finally decided to move to another state to finish school and worked to get residency. He had been smoking marijuana for a few years and now he decided to grow and sell it for extra money. He was heading down a dark path and nothing I said was making a difference. He grew dreadlocks and his hygiene went downhill. He dressed in old torn clothes and wore chains. He carried a pager; all bad signs. When he was at home, he was angry and wouldn't even let me touch him, let alone hug or kiss him. I kept on loving him anyway. I prayed daily that God would intervene in his life and bring him back to us.

Joe bought his first nice car with cash one winter and started home over the mountains with his girlfriend. He had bought the car the day before and hadn't called the insurance company. Taking a curve too fast on the snowy pass, he lost control of the car and totaled it. He and his girlfriend suffered cuts and bruises but miraculously weren't hurt badly. He completely lost his car because of no insurance. We sent him a train ticket to get home to us.

While talking to Joe at home, I told him that I had been praying daily for God to intervene in his life. I was very grateful he had not been hurt badly but I wasn't sorry he had lost his car. I said I believed God had protected him while allowing him to lose a car that was bought with drug money. God would never let go of him and we wouldn't either. We sent him home with my car to borrow until he could get another one and we kept on loving him.

Joe brought his girlfriend home for his sister's wedding the next June and she told me she had introduced him to cocaine and was worried because he really liked it. I wanted to scream at her and I was worried sick about Joe. Before he went home after the wedding, I talked to him about cocaine and of course he told me he was fine and in control. I didn't believe a word of it.

During all these hard years we still saw glimpses of our real Joe underneath the Joe he was trying to be. He was the closest to his little sister Julie, who had cerebral palsy. She championed him and he adored her. He worked an entire day to hook up a "Here Comes the Bride" song on his car horn to play for sister Jenna's wedding. Only Joe called her Jenna and he loved her a lot. He played the song on his horn when she left her reception and it was a highlight of her day because it was such a love gift and such a "Joe" gift. Our boy was still in there and he was worth fighting for.

By November that year, I was so worried about Joe I couldn't sleep. There was nothing different going on that we knew of but something inside me was saying that he was in trouble. I called him regularly and rarely received a call back. I upped my prayers for him, asking God to put a hedge of protection around him to keep evil away. I begged God to send someone to wake him up and bring him back to Himself and to us. By December the urgency I felt about him had grown stronger. I enlisted my husband's help and we started praying out loud together for Joe before bed each night. I begged God to save him in any way He could or would. All six children, including Joe were coming home for Christmas. We were looking forward to having the family time to shower him with love and to talk to him about his life. His sister "Jenna" had been praying for him with me and I knew she would be a big help in getting through to him.

The night before Joe was to come home, my husband and I prayed for him as usual and went to sleep. At three A.M. our phone rang and I lay in bed in total fear as my husband answered it. He was talking to Joe, so thank God, Joe was alive. He was alive and in jail. That night he had gone out with his girlfriend to sell cocaine. Two of his buddies had a cocaine ring going in four states. These guys regularly went to Costa Rica to get the cocaine and bring it home. They had a very successful business going and wanted to branch out into another state so they looked up their good buddy Joe to sell for them. They had just paid him a visit and left a stash of cocaine. This was his first night out to try and sell it. It was stashed under the seat of his girlfriend's pick-up.

As they drove down the street toward their first potential customer, a policeman happened to be behind them and a tail light was out on the truck. The policeman put on his flashing lights and pulled them over. Joe was driving and as he got his wallet out of the glove box to get his license the policeman saw a bunch of cash. He told Joe and his girlfriend to get out of the car and he searched it, finding the cocaine. He questioned them and Joe's girlfriend (the one who introduced him to cocaine) immediately turned on him and told the policeman it was Joe's. Joe was handcuffed and taken to jail.

When my husband told me this in the middle of the night the only thing I could say was, "*Thank you God*." I was filled with more peace than I had experienced in months. I knew without a doubt that God was at work in Joe's life and was going to save him. What are the chances of being pulled over for a tail light the first time you go out to sell cocaine? Joe was in jail and God was definitely working.

Because it was the Christmas holiday, Joe didn't get a hearing until the twenty-sixth of December. That resulted in him spending Christmas Eve and Christmas Day in jail. We called around and found the best defense attorney in his town. We talked to her about Joe and she took his case and went down to the jail to talk to him. He sat in jail for four days thinking about his life, his family who was still there for him and how his drug use had turned out. He lost his drug profits by totaling his car and now he would lose the rest of his money by paying attorney fees. God had not let him enjoy any monetary gain from the drug trade. God and his family were not letting go. He decided he was done with his way of life and especially with the drugs.

His attorney told us that Joe had tried to clean

up in his jail cell before his hearing in front of the judge. He had pulled back his dreadlocks into a ponytail and washed himself up as well as he could. She said he was very respectful and well spoken. She liked him a lot and worked hard to help him. And as God would have it just so we would know without a doubt that this was His hand and His will at work, Joe ended up with no record, not even a misdemeanor. His case was dropped because the truck wasn't his, there was no proof the cocaine was his, and the officer had illegally searched the truck.

That outcome is only good because of the changes that took place in Joe's life and heart. The outcome was God's way of giving Joe another chance and answering our continuous prayers for him. I told him that getting pulled over for a tail light and ending up without a record was God's love for him. His dad told Joe he was disappointed in his actions and if he ever got arrested again, he was on his own. Joe got rid of all marijuana and drugs and never sold them again. Over the next few years, he quit using them all together.

Our son Joe had finally come back to us as the person he was truly meant to be. He had become comfortable with himself after fifteen years of trying to be somebody else. He still had a way to go before being used in a mighty life changing way for the world, as Joseph was used in the Bible, but he had already changed us in a mighty way. We had learned that God will not give up on our children, no matter the circumstances. God can use something as inconsequential as a tail light to achieve His purpose and to answer our prayers. He taught us that as much as we love our Joseph, He loves him more.

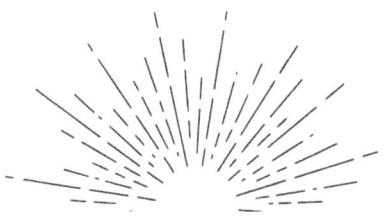

THIRTEEN

Miracle of the Black Angel

After twenty years of prayer, God's gift out smarts three psychologists, one psychiatrist, teachers, friends and Julie's family.

I was on my knees again. It seemed; Julie's cerebral palsy would keep me on them forever. Each year brought new challenges in raising our sweet daughter and this year it was graduation from high school. She was doing great at school, but this was the last year that was planned out for her. Graduation meant starting her adult life and Julie had some challenges. She had a bright mind but her motor skills were a huge stumbling block to securing a job. Her entire body was affected by the cerebral palsy, which meant she couldn't walk or use her arms and hands well. She was great on the computer but very slow typing with one finger. The lack of motor ability in her hands and arms was making it very hard to define a career for her. Just as debilitating as her motor skills was her selective mutism. In the psychiatric textbooks selective mutism falls under the category of social anxiety. In essence it means that the individual is only able to speak to certain people with whom they are comfortable. People with selective mutism have a very difficult time when focused attention is on them, and they get so anxious they truly cannot get any words out of their mouths.

Julie's selective mutism started when she was a toddler. She and her twin sister Molly were both very shy around people outside of our family. Julie got more focused attention because of her cerebral palsy and she couldn't walk away from it like Molly could. Julie was adorable with her little leg braces, glasses and walker. People would stop and ask about her, stare at her, and ask her questions. She just couldn't take it. She was very distrustful of people outside of our immediate family. When we brought her home from the NICU she would only let me and Molly touch her. Anyone else would make her cry. Eventually she opened up to her father and siblings but that is as far as it went.

Julie and Molly each said their first word at eight months of age. They were lying on their backs on my bed after a diaper change. I talked to them constantly, and this day I was asking them their names and then answering for them with either Julie or Molly.

When I asked Molly, "What is your name?" in my best baby voice,

Molly said, "Julie", as plain as could be.

I was shocked and delighted.

I asked Julie, "What is your name?", and waited. She said, "Molly."

Again, it was perfectly clear. I was filled with joy. Their first words were each other's names and Julie had spoken as clearly as Molly! The girls proceeded to pick up words rapidly and by a year of age both of them were saying short phrases, but only their family ever heard them. They were both totally quiet when other people were around. Molly finally started to answer direct questions when she was asked, but Julie couldn't do it. She would look down when strangers spoke to her and she finally progressed to hiding her head under her arms to try to disappear.

Julie's selective mutism made her life harder than her cerebral palsy did. Because she wore leg braces, walked in a walker and wouldn't speak, people assumed she was mentally disabled. They would talk really loud to her like she was deaf and they would ask all kinds of rude questions about her. I felt so sorry for Julie and helpless to help her.

She was such a bright, funny, happy little girl and if she would just talk, other people would know that about her. She made life much more difficult for herself. Molly stood up for her as they got older. The dirty looks she gave to people who were talking down to Julie were almost embarrassing but funny, too. She would look disgusted at them and push Julie away in her wheelchair.

Over the years we took Julie to four different psychologists to try and help her become comfortable speaking outside of our family. The first one said to ignore the fact that she didn't speak and it would go away. We ignored it for eight years and it didn't go away. The second one had a few sessions with her and gave up. The third one ignored her, offered her a hundred dollars to speak to him, had a large knife brought into the therapy room and set on his desk for her to look at, and finally set up a school program for her which the school implemented and turned into abuse. We intervened in the school program, had Julie changed to a new classroom with a loving teacher and the psychologist apologized profusely for his botched attempt at helping her. The fourth psychologist was wonderful, creative, and cracked Julie a little. She understood selective mutism for what it was; a mental illness called social anxiety and not a stubborn streak or something she did for attention and control as others liked to tell us. This psychologist helped Julie learn some age-appropriate social skills for high school. She was fourteen by this time and her social skills were lacking because she had avoided people and not talked to the ones she was around. The psychologist referred Julie to a psychiatrist for medication to help the social anxiety. The medication and counseling sessions combined helped her some and she became able to answer direct questions from her teachers and others, but she still couldn't initiate conversations on her own. It was better than nothing and we were so grateful.

Now the end of high school was here and life was changing drastically. Julie's identical twin Molly was leaving for Cambridge to study abroad and then on to University of Portland for a B.S. in Nursing. Julie would be left at home alone with the "old people". She became more and more depressed as graduation approached. After Molly left, Julie slept in the mornings until I made her get up. She was lethargic and had no interest in things that she had previously enjoyed.

As God would have it, Maryanne Schmidt, a

friend I made at married student housing twenty-eight years earlier, called me out of the blue. She asked about Julie and I told her about how life was changing. Maryanne's second daughter was born with a difficult disability six years earlier than Julie and Maryanne understood what we were facing. She told me about Canine Companions for Independence, a nonprofit organization that trained service dogs for the disabled and hearing impaired. Maryanne's daughter had received her service dog several years earlier and her dog had made a huge difference in her life. CCI, as the organization was called, had shut down their waiting list for dogs five years prior because the list was so long. They had just reopened it and we could apply online at their website. The entire process would be free to Julie. I was so excited to tell her. She was a huge animal lover and this was an opportunity for something wonderful, all her own, to look forward to. We went online together and filled out the first application.

Suddenly I was hit with a lack of faith. I wanted to pray with Julie for her dog, but this was so important to her. I had no trouble trusting God for my needs and desires and continuing to trust Him when answers were a little slow or not what I desired, but I was scared to bring my Julie to Him with a request that was critically important to her.

My fear made no sense. I had already experienced this fear with my oldest daughter when we prayed for her Christmas dress and it arrived on the doorstep! I hadn't totally learned my lesson. God in His mercy and love was willing to teach me the same lesson many times and put up with my wavering faith. I should have been rushing to Him with my children and their prayers. He loved them more than I did, but my mother's heart was so protective. My deepest desire was to have my children come to love and trust God with all their hearts and to experience His constant presence in their lives, and yet I hesitated because what if their prayers weren't answered in the way they hoped? Would their faith be forever shaken? I had struggled with this fear and my need for control ever since my children were born. I was still learning that God is God to all of us, even my children, and He is sovereign over us all. I was still learning that when I held them close in fear, I was slowing their process of finding Him for themselves.

Julie and I prayed together. We asked God to bless this application to CCI and to direct the entire process Julie was undertaking. We asked Him to bless the dog that was to be Julie's, bless the puppy raiser who would raise it and the trainers who would train it. We asked Him to create a dog that would be exactly right for Julie. We prayed this prayer on June 5, 2003 and God took control.

We soon found out that receiving a service dog was like getting into an Ivy League school! Julie received an application which had to be returned with an extensive written essay, three recommendations from non-family members, and a letter from her physician describing her physical limitations and abilities. She returned the application, we prayed for her dog again and waited months for an answer. Finally, she was notified that her application was accepted and the next step was a phone interview. (Remember, she didn't speak, especially on the phone.) We practiced together going over and over possible questions and answers. We prayed for her dog and for the phone interview. A few months later when the phone call was finally set up and the call came through, Julie was able to answer mostly "yes" and "no" to the questions asked of her. I was so scared she would cut herself off from a service dog because of her selective mutism. The CCI interviewer talked to me next and we had a good conversation. She said that Julie would receive a personal interview in Santa Rosa, California if she was selected to proceed further.

We continued to pray for Julie's dog and it seemed to take forever before she received her letter of invitation for her interview. In the meantime, we were building a new house in a neighborhood that was great for Julie's independence. It was in a safe, gated community and had wide paths with no curbs so Julie could someday walk her dog for miles without fear of getting hurt. We installed accessible, dog friendly flooring and planned how she would take care of her dog independently. All this planning gave Julie something to focus on besides her loneliness. When her interview acceptance letter arrived, Julie's smile lit up the room. We made arrangements to drive to California for the interview in early November of 2004.

Again, Julie had trouble speaking. She had to work directly with the dogs and give commands. Julie spoke so softly that the trainers couldn't hear her. The dogs were wonderful and they heard her and followed her commands. We had a follow up interview after the training session and the trainer told us that Julie couldn't be considered for a full-service dog because she was too quiet and timid to control a dog on her own. If Julie made the waiting list at CCI she would be invited to come for assisted service training, meaning that someone would have to be trained with her and would have to go into the public with her and her dog. We went home praying to God that Julie would be put on the waiting list. The letter of acceptance arrived fairly quickly and Julie was thrilled. She could be called to team training in California any time over the next year. We waited and prayed that God would bless her dog. In May of 2005 I called CCI to see where Julie was on the waiting list. Training classes were to be held in May, August and November of that year. I was told that the May training class was full and Julie was next on the list so we could count on August. Julie's sister Jennifer was going to be trained with us because Julie spent time in Seattle with her as well as time at home. If Jennifer was trained to help, Julie could take her dog out in public in Seattle. Jennifer was expecting a baby at the end of May but we had permission to bring the baby to training with us. Our family members started making arrangements to travel to California for Julie's graduation ceremony at the end of team training. We went shopping for new clothes and cleared our schedules for the middle two weeks of August. This was a huge deal in Julie's life.

The first week in August we received a call from CCI telling us that the trainers wanted Julie to wait until November to be trained with her dog. This was devastating news and we wanted to know why. Their reasoning was that Jennifer's baby was too young to go through training, and they would have more dogs trained and ready to choose from in November. After all the plans we had made and as excited as Julie was, this news was hard to swallow. Three more months seemed like an eternity. Julie and I sat down and talked. We had trusted God through this entire process and we needed to keep trusting that He was ultimately in control. We prayed again for the dog that would be Julie's.

Slowly but surely November came. Julie and I made the eight-hour drive down to Santa Rosa, California; the eight-hour drive that turned out to be ten! My husband, who loves maps, had looked at a map and insisted that I take a short cut that would cut out at least an hour of driving. I balked at the idea, wanting to follow the directions sent from CCI. He was adamant that he could save us time in the car. Julie had trouble traveling long distances because of her muscle tone and fused spine. Reducing our time in the car would be beneficial, but I knew I tended to get lost easily and I still trusted CCI's directions. We set off to California and my persistent husband called me twice so I wouldn't miss his exit! Against my better judgment, I took his exit.

Needless to say, it was a big mistake. We traveled on a poorly marked road that wound through a mountain range around hairpin curves. It was extremely dark that night as a horrendous storm was blowing in, a storm that sent so much water pouring out of the sky that I couldn't see through the windshield with the wipers going full blast. As we watched the minutes and then hours tick by on the clock in our car, we realized that we were going to be late (or miss) the first meeting of team training. I reached for my cell phone to call CCI, only to discover that we didn't get service up in these lonely, scary, God forsaken mountains. I wanted to kill my husband! Julie had waited for almost two years to get to CCI team training and she was going to miss the start because he insisted that we take his short cut. I was a nervous wreck by the time we reached CCI headquarters. We walked into the meeting as it was nearing the end, and apologized for being late. I then proceeded to ream out my husband in front of a class of twenty people we didn't even know. I think it broke the ice for the group because everyone seemed to relax and laugh at the trouble Julie's dad was in. That was the start of an amazing training class full of laughter, stories and fun with people we would grow to love.

 CCI provided free housing in their dormitory rooms, all totally accessible for the trainees. We checked into our room and settled in. Jennifer and baby Clara were flying in from Seattle the next day and we would drive to San Francisco to pick them up at the airport. It felt good to crawl into bed that night after the long drive and to finally be at CCI headquarters where we hoped to find a friend and helper for Julie.

The next morning classes started at eight sharp and we found ourselves in a large room with our classmates and two instructors. Ken was extremely skilled and experienced in training CCI dogs. He had been with CCI since its inception and our class gave him the name of Master Yoda. Angie was a level two instructor, was a great communicator and had a smile and laugh that kept us all at ease. They were a winning combination. Yes, God had gone before us.

There were ten trainees in our class. Some had lost their service dogs to old age and were receiving replacement dogs. One was a physical therapist who' would use her dog to motivate children to work on motor skills. We had a special education teacher with a wicked sense of humor whose dog would help calm children with emotional behavioral problems. The trainees had various needs due to cerebral palsy, muscular dystrophy, multiple sclerosis, spinal cord injuries and other debilitating diseases. They were all wonderful. Julie was the youngest at age twenty.

The instructors told us they would spend the first week getting to know each of the students and learning their individual strengths, weaknesses and needs. They knew their dogs well and would work really hard to match the right dog with the right person. They warned the class not to get attached to any certain dog during training because each dog had different strengths and the trainers would be able to choose the right dog for each student. We all attended classes from eight in the morning until about four in the afternoon with an hour lunch break. Some of the classes were with the dogs, learning handling techniques and commands. The others were learning about dogs, how they think, what motivates them, how to care for them and laws pertaining to service dogs.

One of the most important things we learned was pack mentality. Dogs live in packs and one dog is the pack leader. The leader takes care of the other dogs and makes decisions for the pack. They are the dominant dog. Julie would have to do what was needed to become her dog's pack leader. We had homework each night to solidify what we had learned. It was hard work!

The first time the class worked with the dogs, Julie was paired with a dog named Kovin. When Julie gave him the lap command, he put his front legs on her lap and proceeded to kiss her face all over. The entire class laughed and Julie looked extremely happy. As the week passed, Julie's voice grew from a whisper to very quiet which was progress but not enough to change her status from assisted service to full-service dog. Each day Julie would work with a different dog and she loved them all.

When the big day came for receiving the dogs, we went into the training room early to look in the dog crates. There were ten crates lined up with a beautiful dog in each. When the instructors joined us, they had us sit in a circle around the room. They told the class these dogs hadn't been anxiously waiting to meet them like they had been waiting to meet their dog. The dogs wouldn't know them and it would take some time to connect. The dogs were led out of their crates and each leash was handed to their new person. Julie was handed the leash of a female black lab named Teanne. We didn't remember working with Teanne and Teanne wasn't interested in Julie at all. She kept looking around for Julie's instructor, Angie. We didn't know it at the time, but Angie had trained Teanne and Teanne was very bonded to her. One of the reasons Teanne was placed with Julie was because she was so loving and loyal and bonded so well with people.

Julie worked with Teanne the rest of that day and we went back to our room at dinner time. When we got into the room, Teanne stood facing the door wanting to leave. It was so sad. She wanted nothing to do with us. We talked to her and petted her but she wouldn't leave the door. There was a knock on the door and it was Julie's friend from class, Melissa, with her dog, Yukon. When they came into the room Teanne relaxed and began to play with Yukon and interact more with Julie. Seeing that Yukon was in the dorms and not back at the kennel made Teanne feel more secure. Melissa said Yukon had been unhappy in her room, too. The instructors were right. It would take some time.

Julie fed Teanne her dinner, helped brush her and took her for a walk. All these things helped with bonding, but Teanne was still uncomfortable. We discussed Teanne's life and how confusing it must have been to leave her litter, be raised by a puppy raiser who loved her for a year and a half and then left in a kennel with other dogs. She was bonded now to her trainer, Angie, and wanted nothing to do with us. One problem was that Julie couldn't get down on the floor and snuggle and love Teanne. Jennifer and I had to stay away so Teanne wouldn't bond with us. She was to be Julie's very own. Then a brilliant idea surfaced. If Julie couldn't get on the floor, Teanne would have to get up with her. We knew the service dogs had not been allowed on furniture or beds but we didn't care. She was Julie's dog now and Julie needed to be close to her. We got Julie into her bed with the back raised up and she gave Teanne the "Jump" command. Teanne hesitated and looked around at all of us. She wasn't sure what to do because she knew she wasn't supposed to jump up on beds. Julie gave the "Jump" command again with more authority. Teanne couldn't believe her good fortune. She jumped up on the bed and snuggled right into Julie with her head on the pillow. Julie beamed and her new life with a new love began.

The next week of training was spent fine tuning commands with Teanne and watching Julie and Teanne's bond grow. Julie, Jennifer and I had to pass a written test and a community test with Teanne before we could graduate and take her home. The tests took a lot of preparation and Julie was still not talking or giving commands loud enough to be heard. We all passed our tests, however and we reached the end of training.

The night before graduation we attended a fun reception with all the individuals who had raised the puppies in our class. Cindy, Teanne's puppy raiser, was there and we got to hang out with her and hear stories about Teanne. We found out Teanne was supposed to be placed with someone last August. Most of the August class had needed companion dogs so CCI had kept Teanne out because she was too smart to be a companion dog. They wanted to save her for a service dog. Cindy had called CCI very upset when Teanne wasn't placed. She didn't want Teanne to live in the kennels any longer than she had to. When Cindy heard that Julie was supposed to attend training in August but was changed to November, everything fell into place. Cindy cried when we told her that we had prayed for Teanne and her puppy raiser for two years and that we had trusted God for exactly the right service dog. Teanne couldn't be placed in August because Julie wasn't there and it was becoming more and more obvious that they were meant to be together. Cindy gave Julie a baby book and a DVD of Teanne as a puppy and her first year growing up. Julie gave Cindy some thank you gifts for raising Teanne. It was an emotional and very special evening. I could tell that Julie was extremely grateful to Cindy and liked her very much, but she still couldn't get words out except for a thank you.

 The next afternoon Julie handed Teanne over to Cindy so they could spend a last afternoon together while we got ready for graduation. That night, on the stage at the theater, Julie's name was called. She went forward in her wheelchair and Cindy brought Teanne up on the stage and handed Teanne's leash to Julie. Julie and Teanne were officially an assisted service team. We scheduled a mandatory return visit for three months later to retest and make sure everything was going well. We took Teanne home the next morning.

Julie was happier at home. Each day she got up out of bed with excitement to spend time training, exercising, grooming and playing with Teanne. She loved taking Teanne out in public because people didn't stare at her anymore. They were staring at Teanne and that was great because Julie loved showing off her beautiful girl.

One day something happened that changed Julie. We took Teanne to the movie with us. We went to watch "Seven Below", a movie about sled dogs who get left alone in the arctic over the winter months. The movie was very emotional and extremely sad at times. Teanne was lying on the theater floor at Julie's feet when a very sad part came on the screen. One of the sled dogs fell down a cliff and died. His partner sat by his side and cried, nudging him to get up. As the crying continued, Teanne became agitated and stood up. She then proceeded to climb up onto Julie's lap. She hid her head behind Julie's neck. Teanne was treating Julie just like her mommy and wanted to be held and comforted. Julie's face was amazing with emotion for this dog of hers. At that moment Teanne became Julie's child; the only child she could have. Teanne became her reason for living.

As the three months before retesting passed, Julie became more and more confident and assertive with Teanne. She began talking more and louder around people outside of our family. She taught Te, as she called her, to do new commands to be of more help to her. Julie used the "tug" command to have Te help get her coat off and after one arm came out Teanne immediately ran around to the other side and tugged the other sleeve off with no command at all! Julie also taught her to "Go get Nonna" when she needed help, and Te would come find me and take me to Julie. One time when we had company over and I was distracted in the kitchen, Te came to get me and I didn't notice her. She left, went back to Julie's room, picked up Julie's purse and returned to the kitchen with it. She then shook it by my leg at the stove. She definitely got my attention and I was amazed at her problem-solving ability.

About a month before we returned to California, Julie asked if I thought CCI would let her retest with Teanne by herself to become a full-service team. I told her that I didn't know but she could call or email them and ask. I seriously had my doubts about Julie out on her own with Teanne but I didn't want to stifle her confidence or discourage any attempt she made at independence. She emailed CCI and waited for a reply. When their answer came back, she was ecstatic. CCI said they thought it was too early to reach the goal of independent service team but if she wanted to try, they would let her. Now she was motivated and began taking control of her situation. We went to the mall and she would go through all the commands alone with Teanne out in public. One of the tests was the french-fries drop. Julie would sit at a table and drop french-fries on the floor right by Teanne. If Te went for the french-fries, we were literally supposed to dig them out of her mouth or she would fail that test. This was a hard one for Te because she was a lab and she loved her food! If she went for the fries, Julie couldn't get down out of her chair and reach into her mouth. That worried me. I would nervously stand back and watch them. Later, I began hiding around corners as they practiced so Teanne wouldn't even know I was there. They did amazingly well and Julie's confidence grew by leaps and bounds. By the time February rolled around and we were ready to head to California, I was very confident in Julie's ability, but would she talk?

The morning of testing at CCI we talked to Teanne and told her that she would have to be very good for Julie today. She seemed to understand as she looked at us with her intelligent brown eyes. We would see. The students were separated into groups with different trainers for testing. I stood back and heard Angie, Julie's previous trainer, talk to one of the trainers in Julie's group. Angie pointed out Julie and told the trainer to watch her all the time. It was obvious that CCI had qualms about Julie on her own and I felt so nervous for her.

The test started and Julie sat up very straight and confident in her chair. She gave Teanne the "Let's go" command in a loud voice and they took off. Julie and Te did every command perfectly. Julie kept a loud and confident voice throughout the entire test. She accidentally dropped the leash as she was going down the mall and Teanne stopped, picked up the leash in her mouth and returned it to Julie's hand! I saw the trainers watching in excitement about Julie and Teanne's amazing connection. When they got to the french-fries test and Julie dropped them on the ground, Teanne turned her head away from them and acted bored with the whole thing. God bless her! I have never felt so proud in my life as I did while watching my selectively mute daughter give loud commands to her dog out in public with everyone watching her. She and Teanne totally aced the test. They were the best service team present and obviously had a tight bond with each other.

When we met with Julie's original trainers, Ken and Angie, they told Julie she was the first person ever at CCI to pass as an individual service team in only three months with her dog. Julie exploded with pride and excitement. I started to say something and Julie interrupted me with her own thoughts and stories about Teanne. I sat there in disbelief watching the total shock on the trainers faces. They had worked with Julie for two weeks and had not heard her speak a word above a whisper and now we couldn't keep up with all her loud conversation! I had lived with Julie for twenty-one years and had never heard her speak so loudly to anyone outside our family. We were witnessing a miracle. That beautiful, intelligent, intuitive, sensitive, wonderful dog had done for Julie in three months what four psychologists, one psychiatrist, numerous teachers, her friends and her family couldn't do for her in twenty-one years. God had answered my daughter's own prayer in a way we had never imagined. He had more in store for her than we had dreamed possible. He had created a dog for her that would change her life in the very way she had so desperately needed for so long. He gave her back her voice through the answer to her prayer. He sent her Teanne, her very own black angel.

FOURTEEN

The Legal Fiasco and Faith

How God turns an unfair, frustrating, heartbreaking situation into incredible faith.

This story is painful to tell, but I think it needs to be told because through it God changed the focus of my life in a profound way. It concerns our Julie who was hurt by a pediatrician at one day of age in the hospital's neonatal nursery. Julie has cerebral palsy. For eleven years after her birth, we worked with her multiple times each day to help her get strong, walk with a walker and crutches and lead a fairly normal life. She went to school with her twin sister and met all her own daily needs except putting on socks, shoes and braces. I was comfortable leaving her on her own, without a helper for a day at a time. She was doing great.

By age eleven, Julie's femur bones had rotated

inward because of muscle imbalances in her legs. Her knees hit together when she walked and they were slowing her down. During a visit to a children's hospital, a doctor said we should have osteotomies done on Julie's legs to straighten them so that she would walk better throughout her teenage years. An osteotomy is done by cutting the femur bone, rotating it back to a straight position and putting it back together again with metal plates and screws. I was very hesitant to let anyone do surgery on Julie after what had happened to her in the nursery after her birth.

When we left the doctor appointment a physical therapist followed us down the hall to the brace shop. He said that Julie really needed this surgery, the doctor we were seeing was the best at doing it and we would have really good results. He was very insistent about the surgery and told me to strongly consider it.

When we got home, I consulted with the physical therapist at Julie's school. She knew of a couple of kids who had the surgery and who had been able to walk much more easily. My husband and I talked it over and I took Julie back to the children's hospital for another consultation. I talked to the surgeon and told him if we scheduled Julie for the surgery, I would want his word he would do the entire surgery and not let anyone practice on her.

I told him she had cerebral palsy because a doctor had done a surgical procedure on her which he wasn't proficient in and he had done it incorrectly. I told the surgeon I knew children's hospital was a teaching hospital but we had insurance and would go somewhere else if anyone was going to be allowed to practice on Julie. He told us he would do the surgery. He then said Julie was a candidate for adductor muscle lengthening. He thought her tight adductors might be the reason her femur bones had turned inward. He wanted us to go to a gait lab to video Julie's walking pattern and test the tightness of all her muscles before deciding what the surgery would entail.

We made an appointment at the gait lab for a month later. That day was pretty grueling. Julie's entire body was hooked up to electrodes that would send information to a computer to see how her muscles worked together when she moved. She was filmed walking with and without her braces back and forth on a line. She went through multiple tests and measurements to gage the tightness and strength of each muscle. The doctor would use these measurements and information to make decisions about the surgery. We asked the doctor again if he would be doing the entire surgery and he assured us both that he would be.

We drove to Portland the day before Julie's surgery. She needed blood tests and we went through orientation. That evening my husband, Julie and I met with her doctor to sign all the surgery papers. One paper said we authorized the doctor or his assistants to operate on Julie. I balked and reminded him that only he was to do the surgery. He assured us all that he would do the entire surgery and that this was just a standard form. The surgery to be done said bilateral osteotomies and possible adductor releases. I asked him why "possible" releases. He said that he wanted to check the tightness of her muscles under anesthesia before making a decision.

I had read everything I could find on osteotomies and felt comfortable that Julie needed them, but I didn't know about muscle releases because they were mentioned once as a possibility but not really discussed. I asked what the gait lab had indicated about Julie's adductor muscles and he said it was somewhat inconclusive. I feel like I'm going to throw up just writing this. Looking back, I should have been able to see red flags, but I trusted the doctor. In my mind, muscle releases meant stretching them out so they wouldn't be so tight when in actuality it meant cutting completely through the muscle so that it is gone forever. If I had known that, I never would have signed that form. Don't ever just trust a doctor with your child. Don't get rushed into decision making if you need more information. Make sure you know exactly what will be done in a surgery before your loved one ever goes into the operating room. And cross out wording on those permission forms and change things until they say exactly what you are agreeing to. Don't take anyone's word for it.

As you've probably guessed, the surgery was a disaster. The doctor let a resident practice on our Julie. The doctor did the right leg and then let the resident do the left. The right leg ended up to be rotated 20 degrees too far inward. The left leg was rotated outward 40 degrees too far, the bone was cut on an angle rather than straight, and permanent nerve damage was done so that her left leg has remained reddish and blue with poor circulation. Julie lost feeling in it and it will cause her problems as she ages. Because the bone was cut on an angle rather than a straight cut it didn't fit together when it was turned. This meant it was unstable and Julie couldn't bear weight on it for weeks instead of getting up on it right away. The longer she remained down off her feet, the longer her recovery took and the weaker she became.

When we finally returned to the children's

hospital a month later, the physical therapist said we would be so happy at the way Julie would walk now. He told us stories about other children and how excited they were. We went to the PT room and he got her walker. Julie tried to stand up and she collapsed back into the chair. Her legs wouldn't hold her. I looked at her face and the therapist's face and knew something was desperately wrong. We stayed at the hospital for four days and Julie still couldn't stand. We were devastated. I took her home, called our physical therapist who came right over, and we started from the beginning with the simplest exercises to strengthen Julie again.

We made a therapy room at our house and I worked with Julie, doing exercises with her four times every day. The physical therapist came twice a week to update her strengthening program. School was starting and Julie couldn't go and sit every day so I home schooled her, stopping for therapy between each class. With her adductors cut, Julie couldn't even sit up straight, let alone stand or walk. She needed those strong adductor muscles to hold herself upright and counteract her weaker muscles. They were gone forever.

Over the next four months Julie got much of her strength back, but still had trouble walking or standing. She could no longer lift her feet up off the ground, get into or out of bed, get into the car, transfer on or off the toilet, shower or dress herself. She needed my help to do all those things that she had been doing for years on her own. They were all skills dependent on adductors.

One day I noticed that Julie's left hip was raised up off the ground when she was on her back for exercises. I showed the therapist and she said we should go see a new pediatric orthopedic doctor in town. Even with all the therapy Julie had done, she still couldn't walk and now her spine was turning. We made an appointment with the new doctor and our physical therapist went with us.

At the appointment the doctor took a history of Julie and then had me lay her down on the table for an exam. He moved her legs around.

"I can tell you right now why Julie can't walk. Her right leg is rotated twenty degrees too far inward and her left leg is rotated forty degrees too far outward. She can't walk with her legs in this position."

I felt like I had just been punched. He examined her for thirty seconds and knew what was wrong. She had been examined at the children's hospital twice and they didn't say a thing. They had just let her work hard all year trying to walk, knowing she wouldn't be able to do it. I was beyond angry and I felt so sorry for all that Julie was going through.

This new orthopedic doctor told us about Gillette Children's Hospital in St. Paul, Minnesota where he had done his pediatric fellowship. Gillette specialized in cerebral palsy. A physician named Dr. Gage headed up the cerebral palsy clinic. He had a daughter with cerebral palsy and was known as the "cerebral palsy guru." I found Dr. Gage's name on the internet and read about Gillette Hospital. I was interested. Our orthopedic doctor wanted us to go to Gillette and have Julie evaluated at their Gait Lab. He said she would need to have her osteotomies redone as soon as possible because the longer she stayed non-ambulatory the harder it would be for her to regain strength. He also sent us to see a back specialist because she had a curve developing in her back.

We saw the back specialist later that week and found out Julie had a severe seventy-degree curve in her lumbar spine. That was why her hip was raised when she laid on her back. This seventy-degree curve had formed in only five months. We were told Julie needed a spinal fusion to straighten the curve and stabilize her spine. The nightmare just kept getting worse. I told the specialist Julie's hips were turned twenty and forty degrees too far and her adductors were cut. She had lost her stability and her muscles were weakened because she was kept down in a wheelchair so long after

THE LEGAL FIASCO AND FAITH

her surgery. I asked if that would cause Julie's back to curve that rapidly.

The specialist looked at me and said, "That would do it."

I went home and called Gillette Children's Hospital to make an appointment with their gait lab. I also scheduled appointments with a pediatric surgeon for the osteotomies and with one of the best back surgeons in the United States to give us another opinion on Julie's spinal curve. We were to stay at Gillette for a few days and have three evaluations. At our first evaluation we learned the surgeons at Gillette had quit cutting adductors a few years earlier and the children's hospital should have known not to cut Julie's. It was very depressing to hear that information.

Over the next three years we made five flights to Minnesota, stayed in hotels for over a week at a time and supported Julie through four surgeries. She had her osteotomies redone first and they were done perfectly. She had her spine fused six months later. We kept working at home with therapy programs and remained hopeful about standing and walking. Julie's spinal fusion was a huge setback because after the fusion she could no longer twist around or bend over. This spinal surgery made walking, and everything else, much more difficult. She had to relearn every movement.

I stayed in touch with the doctor at Gillette and he called me a year after the spinal fusion. He said he kept trying to think of a way to help Julie overcome her loss of adductors. He had consulted with Dr. Gage because Dr. Gage was "used to cleaning up other people's messes." There was a possibility that with some muscle and tendon transfers they could give Julie enough stability to stand. This would at least allow her to transfer on her own and have a little independence. We were willing to try, so back we went for the last surgery. The muscle transfers helped a little, but everything was still extremely difficult.

After four years of hard work and surgeries, Julie turned fifteen and we were still spending hours each day in our home therapy room. One day when Julie was on her back and we finished an exercise, we looked into each other's eyes. The futility of what we were doing passed between us and we both started to cry. We cried for a long time because we both knew that Julie would never walk again. We would never be able to undo the damage that had been done at the children's hospital. After years of hard diligent work and independence, it had all disappeared in one dishonest and incompetent surgery. Julie's independence was

THE LEGAL FIASCO AND FAITH

gone and her life was drastically changed forever.

Over the next three years, Julie's life was very challenging. Her adjustment to being totally dependent on us for most of her daily needs was painful. Her self-esteem faltered and we saw signs of depression. She asked us repeatedly if we were going to let the children's hospital "get away" with what they had done to her. She was angry and we both felt betrayed by the surgeon who had repeatedly lied to us before and after the surgery. My husband and I didn't know what to do. We didn't like the idea of a lawsuit. We didn't want the stress of it, we couldn't really afford it and we believed in forgiveness. Most of all, it wouldn't bring Julie's independence back or really change anything. Julie kept asking her question about letting them get away with it.

One night when Julie was seventeen, my husband and I had a difficult conversation about her situation. We decided that if it was that important to Julie to pursue restitution for what had been done to her, we needed to do it. We didn't want her asking us thirty years later why we hadn't cared enough to do something about it. We had spent a small fortune flying back and forth to Gillette Children's Hospital trying to undo the damage that had been done to her. Julie was going to need daily care for the rest of her life because of what they did. The hardest of all to deal with was the lies that they had told us; the lies that didn't allow us to care for our girl. With a heavy heart, I started looking for a malpractice attorney.

We found an attorney in Portland who was the brother of one of my husband's friends. He had won some big malpractice cases and he was interested in Julie's case. This attorney carried his Bible with him, and when I went to his office for the initial discovery, he had a wall plaque that had an Old Testament quote about defending the orphans and widows. He took Julie's case against the children's hospital but said he would do the research and decide what avenue to take against them. He wanted us to stay out of it. He also said a law had been passed prohibiting him from bearing the cost of the case. He said that he wouldn't charge for his time unless he won the case and then he would take 40% of the money awarded. The client had to finance the case. I signed a large number of forms to allow him to get information and left it in his hands.

This "Christian" attorney ended up billing us for more money than what he actually spent on the trial, over $20.000 more, and we had been paying interest on that amount on our line of credit. An attorney friend told me client money must be accounted for and returned within a month of closing the case.

THE LEGAL FIASCO AND FAITH

When the trial was over, our attorney didn't find the time to send us an accounting of the money we gave him for eight months. When we looked over the accounting, we saw a charge added on the end of the balance sheet to a name we had never heard of. The charge was for about $4,000 and there was no check number or check date noted for the payment to this mystery person. Our daughter Heidi, who worked in accounting at that time, went over the balance sheets for us. After a couple hours of work, she told us the $4.000 charge had nothing to back it up and we should question it. She also found two other charges within the pages that had nothing to back them up. They totaled over $1,500.

 I immediately called the attorney's office and talked to his assistant who had done the accounting. I had her look at the three charges in question and she said she was sure they were legitimate. I told her I would need information backing all three and I asked her to send it to me. She said she would do it right away. I never heard anything back from her. I called the office a few more times, always leaving a message for the assistant to call me back, but I never received a phone call.

 After a month or so I sent a letter to the attorney asking about the specific charges. I told him I would either need much more explanation about the charges in question, or he would need to refund our $5,500. I asked him to please get back to me promptly. I never heard from him. Finally, after another month passed, I called and made the secretary put me through to the assistant. When she came on the line, she sounded kind of shaky and quiet. I asked why she never got back to me and she said the attorney had sent me a letter explaining the charges. I told her I had never received a letter or communication of any kind. She asked me to hold the line, and when she returned she admitted I was right. No letter had been sent, but the charges were legitimate and the attorney would get back to me. Of course, he never did.

I waited a couple of weeks and then I looked up the phone number to the Oregon Bar Association. When the administrative assistant answered, I explained what was happening to me and she gave my information to the attorney in charge of policing other attorneys. He called me back and recorded the details of what had been going on since our trial ended. He told me I had every reason to be upset with our attorney and he was upset with him, also. He told me he would take care of the situation.

He called our attorney's office that day and was told our attorney was out of the office. He left a message and, interestingly, our attorney called him back within fifteen minutes. They had a little chat

THE LEGAL FIASCO AND FAITH

and our attorney said he would send us a check for the money that was being disputed. I thought the ordeal was over, but we didn't receive the check. I had to call the Bar Association again, they called our attorney again, and we finally received our money back. Our attorney had kept our money for an entire year while we were paying interest on it. It took two calls from the Oregon Bar Association to finally get it back.

I am convinced our attorney would never have sent our money back. We learned that just because he carried a bible and professed Christianity it didn't mean he knew or followed Christ. He turned out to be just as dishonest and incompetent as the children's hospital surgeon. The money fiasco was really the least of the ways he hurt us though. He was completely incompetent in the trial. In fact, the whole trial was a joke. Let's back up.

When our attorney started investigating Julie's case, he went out to Gillette Hospital and spoke with Dr. Gage, the cerebral palsy guru who has written books on cerebral palsy for other doctors. Our attorney said Dr. Gage told him that cutting Julie's adductors was the critical mistake in making her dependent for life. He also told our attorney that cutting her bone at an angle and thus keeping her off her feet for six weeks was very harmful to her. He offered to be a witness in Julie's trial. Did our attorney listen to and use Dr. Gage's help? No. He proceeded to find a witness in California who said that using a gait lab was responsible for the mistakes being done during the surgery, and he decided that was the way to go with Julie's trial. It was completely the wrong premise. For every doctor who was opposed to using gait labs, there were fifty who supported their use. If gait labs were used correctly, we supported them also,

Our attorney did find one intelligent witness who understood what had happened to Julie. He was a brain and cerebral palsy specialist who testified that with Julie's athetoid cerebral palsy, the adductor muscles should never have been cut and the children's hospital surgeon should have known that. He equated cutting those adductor muscles to giving a patient penicillin who was allergic to it and causing their death.

Another witness he used was a monetary specialist who projected out how much money Julie would need to meet her needs because of what had been done to her. They came up with an insane amount of money. I can't even remember how many millions they asked for, but it was totally embarrassing to us. It was obviously about the money for our attorney, but it was never about the money for us. We wanted to defend Julie. We knew that no amount of money would ever really help her or regain her loss.

THE LEGAL FIASCO AND FAITH

Before the trial began, we had a deposition for gathering of information. Our "Christian" attorney was so arrogant and disrespectful to the other attorney I could hardly stand to be in the room with him. It was as if a big game of ego had started being played and Julie had nothing to do with it. That was the beginning of my education about the legal system, and it only got worse.

If I had known in the beginning that the defense would keep me from telling the jury everything the other doctors had said about the children's hospital surgery, and known that my own attorney would not be using Dr. Gage as a reputable and critical witness for Julie, I never would have pursued the lawsuit. The jury never heard all the compelling evidence against the children's hospital surgeon:

1. They should have known not to cut adductors; it was an outdated procedure.
2. They shouldn't have lied to me about who was doing the surgery.
3. They shouldn't have kept Julie down for weeks after the surgery.
4. They should have told us immediately that her legs were turned incorrectly.
5. Her botched osteotomies and loss of muscular strength caused her severe spinal curve.

6. Her gait lab results didn't show any reason to cut the adductor muscles.
7. The doctors at Gillette Children's Hospital told me they had lots of experience in cleaning up other people's messes. In other words, the surgeon at the children's hospital had made a mess of Julie's surgery and body.

I was under the impression that a trial was to reveal the truth about a situation and get justice for the party who had been wronged. I was so naïve. The court did not care whether the truth was told to the jury. It became a game of attorneys trying to block each other at every turn in order to win. Julie was completely lost in the process.

Even without being able to share what I knew, our attorney had chances to show the incompetence of the children's hospital surgeon, but he was so clueless as to the basics of the case that he let all his chances go by. For example, a children's hospital witness, who worked in the gait lab and measured muscle tightness on a scale of one to five before surgeries, said Julie's adductors measured a three during her exam. Their attorney, who also didn't understand the case, asked at what point a decision to cut muscles occurred. Their witness said at a measurement of four or five. I couldn't believe it! They had just proved our case. I immediately whispered to our attorney to call them on it. Julie only measured a three in tightness, not enough to consider cutting and they had cut her muscles! Our attorney made no comment. He did nothing. On cross examination he didn't even mention the measure of three out of five on the adductors. The children's hospital also had a witness who backed our case about the surgery causing the spinal curvature. Again, I tried to quickly tell our attorney and he just let it go. It was beyond frustrating.

Our daughter Jennifer is an occupational therapist and her husband is a physical therapist. They took the gait lab records and spent hours going over them and making notes about how those records showed in numerous ways that Julie needed her adductor strength and those muscles should never have been cut. They gave all those notes to our attorney and I don't know if he ever looked at them, but he certainly never mentioned them or used the information.

In the meantime, the defense brought in witnesses who told complete lies about Julie's condition before the surgery and they were allowed their lies because our attorney didn't challenge them. They could lie but I was blocked from telling the truth. The defense attorney didn't like me because when she cross examined me, I was able to say some truths about the case that she didn't want the jury to hear, and that made her mad. She attacked me personally many times when the jury was out of the room, so much so that the judge finally called her off and defended me. When the closing statements came for the trial, though, she stood there and told the jury she knew they all liked me and that she really liked me too, but they needed to decide on proof of facts. They didn't know the facts!

Our attorney got up there in his closing statement and gave some lame talk about Julie's day in court and then he threw some Bible verses at the jury. We could actually see them squirm. It was a perfect ending to the nightmare job he had done.

The night before the closing statements our family was all together in Portland. We talked about the trial and I told them that if I was on the jury, I would not find in favor of Julie. I told Julie the way the courts worked and the way our attorney had handled the trial left the truth of her case untold. We assured her it wasn't fair or right but it was the reality of the situation. Our family had spent $70,000 out of pocket which was sitting on our line of credit because we had believed so strongly in trying to defend her. We told the children that we weren't sorry we had gone through with the trial for Julie. Even though it hadn't gone well, it was

THE LEGAL FIASCO AND FAITH

something we had to do.

I also told them by putting the children's hospital surgeon through the trial we had surely saved other children from the same treatment Julie had been given. We had made him face Julie and what his lies and incompetent decisions had done to her life. I was sure he was going to think through his decisions more thoroughly and not cut adductors again. We all decided that if our seventy thousand dollars saved just one child from losing his or her independence, it would be money well spent. We will never know how many children that trial may have affected but we have to believe some good came out of it because we entered into it with a lot of prayer, believing it was God's will to support Julie.

Getting out of bed the morning following closing statements, I was totally tied in knots. I was extremely restless and worn out. Thinking about going back into that courtroom with all my pent-up frustration was killing me. I went away to an empty room and knelt down by the bed with my Bible. I poured my heart out to God and asked Him to please help me. I explained to Him how we had tried to honor Him and do the right thing for our daughter and we wanted to end all of this in His will. I asked Him to please take the trial and turn it into good for Julie. I told Him I needed a word from Him before we went back to the courthouse.

Then I closed my eyes and opened my Bible with expectant faith. When I looked down at the open page, I was in the Gospel of Luke, chapter 18. I started to read:

> "Then Jesus told his disciples a parable to show them that they should always pray and not give up. He said: "In a certain town there was a judge who neither feared God or cared about men. And there was a widow in that town who kept coming to him with the plea, 'Grant me justice against my adversary.'
>
> "For some time he refused. But finally, he said to himself, 'Even though I don't fear God or care about men, yet because this widow keeps bothering me, I will see that she gets justice, so that she won't eventually wear me out with her coming!"
>
> And the Lord said, "Listen to what the unjust judge says. And will not God bring about justice for his chosen ones, who cry out to him day and night? Will he keep putting them off? I tell you; he will see that they get justice, and quickly. However, when the Son of Man comes, will he find faith on the earth?"

I got excited when I started reading the parable. It was about a judge and justice, just like what we were going through. What were the chances that I would open my bible to that particular page in Luke and that parable? But it was the last line that made my heart jump. It was the last line that sounded loud and clear with God's Holy voice. I had heard this parable before but I had no recollection of the last line in it. It hit me hard. I got chills all over my body. The Lord had spoken. Of course, the parable was fitting for Julie's situation that day. It was about a judge who was being pestered repeatedly by a widow for justice. For six years Julie had repeatedly cried out to God for justice. The parable assured me without a doubt that Julie would receive justice. Maybe not today, but she would receive it. God did not lie and I trusted His answer. But it was not the parable itself that changed me. It was that last line.

"However, when the Son of Man comes, will he find faith on the earth?"

What was that line doing in the parable? It didn't seem to belong there. Why was the Lord asking if He would find faith on the earth when He had just given a lesson on His Father's justice? I could have sworn that last line had added itself just for me at the moment I read it. That was the message God was giving me. It was not what I was looking for, but it cut straight to the heart of the entire trial and ordeal we were going through. I knew what the jury's verdict would be and it didn't matter; our faith mattered. I knew Julie would need help for the rest of her life and it didn't matter; our faith mattered. I knew the attorneys had played their game and made a mockery out of Julie's pain and it didn't matter; our faith mattered. I knew some of the witnesses had lied under oath and it didn't matter; our faith mattered. My heart was filled with a joy that didn't make any sense in the circumstances. Again, God had answered my prayer in a mighty way. He told me Julie would get justice, but He told me what really mattered was that when Jesus returns, He will find us faithful. I was looking at an earthly matter through earthly eyes and God wanted to teach me to look at the higher spiritual matter with spiritual eyes. He loved me enough to teach me to focus on His eternal ways rather than to focus on my earthly sense of right and wrong, good and bad; or earthly justice.

To this day I am still in awe and I still rejoice in the lesson God taught me through Julie's pain and that trial. He taught me that circumstances will come and go and I can count on Him for justice. But more than justice, God cares about my faith, the faith that will bring me to Him and to eternal life. *"However, when the Son of Man comes, will he find faith on the earth?"*

Yes, He will find us faithful.

FIFTEEN

Never Ending Houses

Given to God, my sinful obsession over houses, leads me to entering dozens of new front doors.

In a way, houses have defined my life. They are a constant reminder of my relationship with God. During my fourth pregnancy, I was obsessed with them. Our house was 1200 square feet including a large cement laundry room that had become a playroom, and a decent-sized storage room that was our two-year-old's bedroom. That left very little square footage for the kitchen, dining table, living room, two bedrooms and one bathroom. I was having trouble figuring out where to put the baby who would be arriving in six months. I liked my little house and we were certainly happy there (it had a great big yard), but having more room wasn't something I just wanted. It had become a real need. True to form I set out to find a bigger house.

I assessed the obstacles I was facing. The first, foremost and probably only real obstacle was the fact that we couldn't afford a larger house payment. During that time, we were cutting every monetary corner available and still barely living paycheck to paycheck. My husband Jerry's salary for his summer job at the park needed to be used for emergencies during the year. I needed to find a larger home to buy for the same price that we could sell our home for. This was 1981 and the internet was not an option for locating properties, so I began driving around looking for "for sale" signs. I would write down telephone numbers, return home and make calls. Every price was too high. Not one to be discouraged, I kept driving each day and started looking for rental signs. I thought if God led me to the right house, the owner would surely want to sell us their house for a low price rather than rent it to us. I was driving all over town with three young children, ages five, four and two with me. They hated it! They got fussy and whiny but I just kept driving. I was on a mission and nothing would stop me.

Finally, I found the house! It was in the school area my husband taught in, it was two stories high, had four bedrooms and two bathrooms and was on a safe street for the children. I was so excited. It was for rent but I just knew the owners would sell it to us for the right price. I drove my husband over to see it and he agreed that I could call. I called the number and talked to the owner. He was interested but needed to think about it. He would call me back. I told the children about the house and that it had two bathrooms. They got excited. When the owner called me, he said they had decided to keep it as a rental but they would save our name and number. If they decided to sell it, he would call us first. I thanked him, felt depressed and loaded the kids in the car to start driving again. About an hour into our drive, and way past their nap time, they were all crying in the back seat. I pulled the car over, turned to look at them and a wave of self-loathing swept over me. I was staring at the three sweetest, usually happiest children in the world. I was their mother. I was supposed to meet their needs, but I had reduced them to this. I immediately turned the car toward home. When we arrived at our house, I apologized to them for the constant driving around and told them we wouldn't be looking for houses any longer. I told them when our new baby was born, we would find a spot for him or her to sleep. Mommy had decided that this house was just fine for us. They all looked so relieved.

 I put them down for naps, went to the living

room, got down on my knees and began to literally cry out to God. I was so ashamed. I had been driving around for days and days at the expense of my children, certain I was in God's will. Well, I wasn't, and that was crystal clear to me now. I had made my entire family miserable while trying to solve our crowded conditions on my own. I confessed my obsession as the sin that it was to a very loving and understanding God. I was so sorry and to prove it to Him I made a deal. I told God I was finished with houses forever. I would never care where I lived or what my home was like again. I would use my home searching energy to love and serve God and my family. In fact, I told God if He ever wanted me to move to a different house, He would have to work through my husband. I wanted no part of it!

Looking back, I was making the rules again but God knows me and my heart. He knew I was totally sincere and He honored my prayer even if I was telling Him what to do. I received an amazing peace and joy from that prayer and truthful encounter with God. Houses were gone, gone, gone. I was free to trust God and love my family again. I have had nothing but houses since!

Within two weeks, my husband brought up houses. I kept my mouth shut. He said he had been thinking and he thought we should add on to our house. What did I think?

That thought had never occurred to me, but we had a half-acre to work with and it was a brilliant idea. I told him it was completely up to him what we did about our house situation and I would support anything he decided. I think my answer shocked him. I was not the same maniac he had been living with two weeks ago, and I had not told anyone about my surrender of my will to God. We still had the money problem but I bit my tongue and didn't mention it. I had given it up and it looked like God was going to honor my surrender and work through my husband. I totally loved them both!

Two months before our baby was born, our five hundred square foot addition was finished. We had added a family room, deck, bedroom and bathroom and it was, of course, perfect. My husband had received financing from his grandmother. Friends and family had helped with plans, drawings and permits, plumbing, framing, drywall, and roofing. We had hired the rest and did the entire project for $6,000. I spent the summer playing with the kids, taking them on excursions around Portland and swimming at the park. We had a wonderful summer. I stayed completely out of the building plans and the entire project. Only when my husband asked me to go pick out floors or paint color did I help, and I picked them quickly and within budget. But God knew the desires of my heart. When my husband went to pick out a sliding glass door that would open from the family room to the deck, there just happened to be a real wood French double door unit that had been returned. He purchased it for the same price the sliding door would have cost. When he went to order windows, the owner showed him a beautiful bay window that had been returned and had been sitting in their shop for months. How would we like it for the same price as the one we were ordering? French doors and bay windows were totally out of our budget but made our home look so cozy, not to mention the light they gave to our family room on rainy days. God always gives more than we imagine when we trust Him. We lived comfortably and happily in our home for three and a half years and then the twins were born.

When we brought the twins home, we had a crib in our bedroom and a bassinet in the living room. They were preemies and small enough to share a bed, plus they were happier sleeping together. We had two people in each of our three small bedrooms and it was obvious the twins were without a room, but we were happy and there was no way I was getting dragged into worrying about houses. It wasn't too many months before my husband came home and told me he had found a lot for sale by owner in his school's area. He said he thought we should build a new house.

I said, "Really?" And then I added, "Great!"

The fact that he had no contracting background, and we still had no extra money but now had eight mouths to feed, didn't escape me. But I had given up houses and asked God to work through my husband. I had to trust.

We put our little house on the market "For Sale by Owner". We needed to sell it before we could buy the lot and begin building. In order to sell our home, it had to look its best. That meant it must be clean, toys picked up, beds made, dishes done, etc. I had six children, ages nine, seven, five, three and two infants. I wasn't sure how in the world I was going to take care of my precious little ones while maintaining a perfectly clean and orderly house. Because of the promise I had made to God, I couldn't tell my husband that this plan of his was impossible for me to do. I had to go with his plan for our housing situation, so my only option was to ask God for His help in keeping my promise to Him. How crazy was that? I couldn't even keep a promise to God without Him helping me keep it! I told Him I absolutely couldn't keep my house in perfect order all the time without becoming a less than desirable mother to my children. I told Him if this really was His will and I trusted that it was, then He would have to clean and sell my house Himself!

My little sister had given me a gift after our twins came home from the hospital. She had hired cleaning ladies to come once a week for three months and clean for me. It was a thoughtful, practical, kind and most appreciated gift. Shortly after we put our "For Sale" sign out in our yard, we got a call from a guy wanting to look at the house. He asked if he could come by on Wednesday at four in the afternoon. My husband arranged to be home to show the house. As God would have it, the cleaning ladies also came on Wednesday afternoons. They literally walked out of my house and passed the guy on the walkway as he walked to the front door. The house was spotless and I hadn't cleaned it. The guy bought the house and it turned out he was a committed Christian and we later became friends. God had done what I thought was impossible. He had cleaned and sold my house to let me know without a doubt that this was His will for us. I could trust Him, and again he gave us an extra blessing, a new Christian friend whose life would intersect with ours in interesting ways for years to come.

When we sold our house, we set the closing for two months out. We used Jerry's older brother's contractor's license and somehow got a construction loan. I stayed out of the planning, even letting my husband pick the house plan. We ran into problems with the type of septic system we had to install on our lot, and with our buyer's slow Veteran's loan coming through, but by the grace of God my husband built a 2,500 square foot house in ten weeks. Thinking back, it was a miracle. I don't know how he did it, but it was the only way to make the money work between the construction and permanent loans, so it was done. We moved into a beautiful new five bedroom, two and a half bath home with a double garage on over a half an acre of land. I had never imagined living in a new house and I appreciated it but didn't get attached. I had truly given up houses.

Ten months later we had to move. Jerry had been hired as head football coach where my parents lived in Redmond, Oregon. We were excited, but this was the late 80's and houses weren't selling well. We had to sell. We ended up with a sale that would have to close within a year. My husband went across the mountains to find a rental house that we could afford. He rented a house with three tiny bedrooms and we packed in.

One bedroom had a set of bunk beds and two cribs. There was a two and a half-foot strip of floor space down the middle to walk. Our bedroom had so many children's dressers in it we had to walk in side-ways and could barely get into the closet. We were so happy there. It was one of our best years. We joined Saint Thomas parish where Father Bernard Keating was the priest in charge. He was a loving, godly man and a good teacher. We became friends and he loved having dinner with us and being with all our children. We had football parties, birthday parties, overnights and many friends came to stay with us from over the mountain. We slept them in sleeping bags on the floor and on two couches. Nobody complained. We even had Jerry's brother, wife and four children at Christmas and it was wonderful. Why had I ever thought we needed so much space? We really "needed" very little.

During that year we discovered seven acres on a hillside that looked up at seven mountains in the Cascade Range, and looked down on fields of grazing cattle and horses. It already had a well and an access road, and electricity hook-up was in place. It had been for sale for a long time and had recently dropped off the real estate listing. We offered twenty thousand dollars and bought the seven acres! Jerry started working on house plans. Money was scarce so he designed a house that could be heated with a wood stove in the middle and had one bedroom downstairs in case our Julie (who had cerebral palsy) needed it. In order to afford this house, we would have to do much of the work ourselves.

We went to the building site in the evenings with all six children. We had a crib set up for the twins and the other children slept in sleeping bags. Jerry and I would work until three in the morning and then load everyone up and take them home. It was crazy, but we had to do it to get into our house. We kept up this schedule until Jerry pounded a wood floor nail into his hand and ended up in the emergency room. He could no longer work and we were so close to finishing. Our new friends rallied together, had work parties and finished the house for us. We gratefully moved in. The house had a gambrel roof and cedar siding and looked like a log barn from a distance. We loved it and the boys especially loved the seven acres to explore. The kitchen and family room windows looked up at the mountains and down on the green fields with the horses and cows. It was our little piece of heaven.

We spent three wonderful years in our gambrel house on the hill before we had to move again. Our town was having school budget problems. Buses had been cut so I was driving four children to three different schools, dragging the twins with me. Jerry had to fund raise to support the entire football program. He also had to coach three sports to make ends meet and there was no teaching pay raise in sight. With all his obligations, he was almost never home to help with the six children. The boys were getting older and really needed some time with him, and Julie's cerebral palsy was turning out to be very expensive with doctor appointments, therapy and equipment to buy. We couldn't make it through a month financially, the kids desperately needed clothes and shoes and our cars were almost not running. Jerry loved his job but he started looking for one in business where he could make more money. His new job led us back to our old home town. We sold our little piece of heaven and moved back over the mountain into another rental house.

 As wonderful as those seven acres looking at the mountains were, I never looked back. I was not living for houses. I was living for God and He was in control. We found another large lot for sale by owner and started building. Jerry had drawn up a house plan that would meet our family's needs. We now knew Julie needed to be on one floor with her walker, so only four bedrooms and two bathrooms were upstairs for the rest of us.

 Again, I stayed totally out of the building process, only picking out a few items when asked. It turned out beautifully and was just what we needed. The twins were four years old when we moved into that house just before Christmas. With six children in tow, we had moved five times and built three houses in less than five years. When I let God take over my house fixation, I had no idea what I was getting into. It seemed our lives had become moving and houses, yet I had remained free to care for my family in the midst of it all.

    For six years we remained in one house. It holds wonderful memories of the children growing up there. Eventually, Jerry's corporation did what corporations do. They combined a failing company with his productive one and it took them both down. When it came time for him to lay himself off, (he was the Human Resources director), we were in much better financial shape than we had been six years earlier. He missed teaching and coaching and thought he could return to it if he built one spec house each year to sell. We had one daughter in college and another starting in the fall. I wasn't sure we could make teaching work financially and building a house a year sounded awful to me, but I had asked God to work through my husband so I kept my mouth shut. We moved back over the mountain to Central Oregon where my husband took a teaching and coaching job.

We immediately bought two large lots in a great neighborhood, one for us and one for a spec house. This time I ended up living in a brand new 5,000 square foot house with six bedrooms. I don't think any of us really liked it. It was a very nice house, but we spent all our time in the kitchen and family area. We hardly ever stepped into the living room and the bonus room was rarely used. We liked being together and the space was wasted on us.

We only lived there for a year and a half before we sold the house and built a smaller one. In doing so, we finally got rid of our house loan and could afford to live on Jerry's teaching salary. He continued to build one or two houses a year and each of them sold within four to eight weeks for very fair prices. The house building money paid for college for five children, weddings, Julie's surgeries in Minnesota and family vacations. It paid off cars and allowed us to help our children when they needed help. It allowed us to fly to college football games and watch our son Tommy play linebacker. Jerry built three houses for us and twelve for other people during those years.

I let him run his business and stayed out of it except for one time. I am ashamed to say I stepped in and pushed for the floor plan of a house to be flipped, or repositioned on the lot, so it would have a better view. I couldn't understand why my husband couldn't see that I was right. He was worried that if we flipped the floor plan, there wouldn't be enough space for the driveway. I assured him there would be. That particular house went on the market on September 11, 2001, the day the Twin Towers fell and our lives changed forever. Everything came to a standstill and houses were not selling. I wish I could say that is why our house didn't sell. No, it was because of the driveway. Because the floor plan had been flipped, the driveway ended up steep and awkward. There was very little room to back out of the garage before hitting a rock wall. We had three potential buyers who all loved the house but dropped out because of the driveway. I had broken my promise, opened my mouth about that house, and we were literally paying for it. I wouldn't have bought that house either. We carried the loan on it, making payments for eight months before we ran out of money.

Our second daughter was getting married in June of that year and in May we no longer had enough savings to make the house payment, let alone pay for her wedding. We had dear friends, Hector and Therese, who had called us in September and offered to loan us money if our house didn't sell. We assured them that we would be fine. But on the first of May, which happened to be Hector's birthday, I called and told him that we had a present for him.

Hector hated presents and he started grumbling at me about not wanting a present for his birthday. I told him this present was something he would like; he could loan us money. Well, that made his day! He was excited to do it for us and we made another payment on the spec house. That house sold two weeks later, in spite of the driveway, and it closed just in time for our daughter's wedding. My disobedience had cost us a lot of money that year, but I know God forgave me and my husband did too. I have truly stayed out of houses ever since, but I wasn't the only one God would mold for His purpose by using houses.

One of the houses Jerry built was for a great couple who had a nice lot in a golf course neighborhood. Jerry loved working on that house. He liked the neighborhood setting, all the open green space of the golf course, the wide paved walking paths and the gates that closed it in at night for safety. He came home and began talking about the wonderful neighborhood and how friendly the people were. I could tell he had a plan brewing. It didn't take long before he was broaching the subject of moving again. He wanted to sell our house and buy a lot in the Awbrey Glen golf community. A golf community didn't sound like my cup of tea. Golf was expensive, took lots of time away from home and it was for retired people. None of that described our situation or met our needs, but he persisted. However, Julie was close to receiving her service dog, and she couldn't get out and walk her dog independently in our neighborhood because of all the steep hills and no sidewalks. Because of that, and because I had promised to leave houses to my husband, I agreed to look at the neighborhood.

It was pretty; lots of trees, large lots and the pathways were perfect. I liked it, but the lots were very expensive. If we moved, we might have a house loan again. I could tell Jerry had already moved us into that neighborhood in his head, so Julie and I started driving through it once in a while watching for "for sale" signs. It didn't take long before the perfect lot came up for sale at an amazing price. I told my husband about it and within forty-eight hours we owned that lot.

Here we went again: another house to sell, house plan to figure out, rental to find and move into and all the work. This time our oldest daughter and her two little girls were living with us, so we had to find a rental to hold both families and one that would accommodate Julie's wheelchair. I prayed. If this was what God wanted, He would have to work it out. Of course, He did. I was driving home from taking our oldest granddaughter, Darien, to school and her big eyed four-year-old sister, Monica, was with me. I started to pass an older neighborhood on the left that I had never been in. A voice in my head said, "Go in and look for a rental." I was stunned and kind of scared.

I said to Monica, "Do you think we should go into that neighborhood and look for a rental house?

Of course, she said, "Yes!"

I turned the car around, went back to the neighborhood and drove in. There was the house! Only two steps up to the door for the wheelchair, a large yard, double garage for storage, and the rent was three hundred dollars less than anything else I had found. I went home and called immediately. The lady at the rental firm said she was showing the house later that day, but if I wanted to meet her at 10 AM she would let me in. I was there and it was perfect. It had an entire downstairs for our daughter and her girls, a large master bedroom for Julie with a roll under counter in the bathroom and an accessible shower. I signed papers for the rental house on the spot, and Monica and I sang all the way home. Our house sold the next day. What if I hadn't listened to that voice and obeyed? There sat the perfect rental house for a family with tough and specific needs and it would have been gone that afternoon. It was vacant and ready to live in and we needed it immediately.

Just before we moved in to our Awbrey Glen house, we received a large amount of money from an attorney who had owed it to us. My husband loved to golf and with six children he had maybe golfed ten times in twenty-nine years. Julie and I put our heads together and decided to surprise Jerry with a golf membership. He was thrilled and promptly bought me some golf clubs. That was the beginning of the first difficult time in our marriage.

For the next three years, Jerry built houses, sold them and played golf. That was kind of okay but he was gone an awful lot on the golf course and Julie and I missed him. The worst thing was that he wanted me to join the golfing lifestyle. I wanted him to be happy but I had no desire to make golf an important part of my life. I just couldn't live for golf. I lived for God. I had been living for God since Jerry met me. I hadn't changed. I desperately wanted to commit to attending church. We had tried a few times, but Jerry would never commit and he would miss services because he had a golf game. I began to feel resentful toward him. It seemed to me that we suddenly wanted different things in life and I couldn't believe it. I spent every day taking care of Julie alone and he golfed and built houses. I talked to him about my feelings and he seemed to listen and said he would help me, but things never changed. I became increasingly unhappy.

God stepped in. Jerry had been so successful with building that he decided to do two building projects in one year rather than one. He was thinking about retirement and I know he wanted to take part in the golf tournaments with his retired friends. Teaching was preventing him from doing that. He bought a lot that I thought was foolish and too expensive. I cautioned him once and then let it go. It was his business after all and I had a promise to keep. Meanwhile another lot we had been watching came on the market and it was a decent deal, so he bought it for the next project. He took out a construction loan and started the second house before winter that year.

During the winter, Jerry decided to buy a lot for the third house. Now I said something. Was he crazy? We didn't have the money to support three projects at once. The lot he wanted to buy was outrageously priced and it wasn't even a nice lot. I vehemently voiced my concerns. He told me that without risk there was no gain. He reminded me that he had done very well for twenty-two years and I needed to trust him. I prayed to God to help me and I kept my mouth shut. I felt sick to my stomach when I signed the escrow papers on that last lot. I told Jerry I didn't want to sign it. I even threw the pen across the room at the title company, but we became the proud owners of a lot that was worth $100,000 less than we paid for it.

To get a little off track, there is something I would like to share here. Back when we were having our babies, we received numerous comments from friends and family about the cost of raising them all. Jerry and I had prayed and trusted God with the size of our family. We sincerely wanted to glorify Him in our family life and wanted to have each child that He wanted us to bring into His world. We prayed together and asked God to bless and help us provide for the children He gave us. When I gave up houses, I had no idea that particular surrender would be the source of His provision. Jerry built and sold houses from the time the twins were born until the housing market took a dive in the spring of 2007. That was also the time our last child, Molly, graduated from college and we no longer "needed" the extra money. Interesting timing!

The first of three houses was ready to sell that spring of 2007. Jerry tried to sell it on his own at winter's going rate and it sat for two months. I said to lower the price but he couldn't give up his retirement dream and persisted at the same asking price. He finally hired a realtor and listed it lower but still too high. I looked at competing properties with the realtor, came home and told Jerry to lower the price. He said he couldn't lower it and still make money. Meanwhile, each month housing prices kept dropping. Now the second house was ready to sell. He listed it too high also and it sat. It was a great house and had lots of lookers. In fact, it was the first choice for three buyers but they all decided to wait and see if prices would keep falling. When October rolled around the houses still hadn't sold. We had more than ten thousand dollars a month in two house payments and a payment on a disastrous lot. On November first we would no longer be able to make the payments. We could have weathered a long drought with one house payment but three were killing us. Jerry came to me and asked how much I thought we should lower the house prices. We lowered them. The first one sold and closed exactly on November first, God's timing for sure. That one had His fingerprints all over it. We had lost ninety thousand dollars and we felt lucky and blessed to sell it at all.

    When that house sold, I went to God and asked Him to show me what I needed to learn from this experience. I realized my anger toward Jerry and the house situation stemmed from my pride. Jerry wouldn't listen to me and I thought I knew better. I thought he should have listened and not kept telling me I was being doomsday and negative. I wasn't. I was trying to be smart and jump ahead of the market to sell those houses. But my eyes weren't on God. I wasn't listening for His voice because I was too busy being angry at my husband for not listening to me. When I got my focus back on God and realized that it was okay to lose everything material, the house sold. The second house sold seven months later at a hundred and forty thousand drop in price and a seventy thousand dollar loss. Because we couldn't sell the lot (it was kind of becoming a joke now) without losing at least another hundred thousand dollars, and we probably couldn't sell it at all, we were forced to sell our home for a low price and rebuild our home on that lot. We needed to build for us again and I was going to have to live on the very piece of land I had fought so hard against.

While we were selling our home, I was living with a very humble husband. He apologized for not listening to me and for making such poor decisions. We started back to church, and the fellowship and eucharist were healing for us and our marriage.

Our house sold and then fell through two days before closing. We lost money on a rental deposit and were frustrated. I got back on my knees in the bedroom and prayed for God to keep teaching me what I was missing in all of this. I didn't get the answer for days, but I kept asking and listening with a true heart and He hit me with it one afternoon. I could have no other gods before Him. In the past I had made my children my god and had worked through that, but I had never completely given up my husband. Jerry and I had been together since we were sixteen and I adored him. He was the best guy I had ever known and I expected him to be perfect and make everything okay for me all the time. I had put him in God's place and it wasn't fair to him.

I had always heard that God was a jealous God and we were to have no other gods before Him. Those thoughts had always bothered me because the God I knew was so loving and wise and I couldn't imagine Him being jealous of any love in my life. But now I saw it all another way. What if we were to have no other gods before him because it wasn't fair or good for the object of our love or for us? By putting Jerry on a pedestal, I was putting a lot of pressure on him to be perfect and he couldn't live up to that forever. Nobody could meet my every need and be completely trustworthy for me except the real living God. I was setting my husband and myself up for failure and disappointment just like I set up my relationship with my children for many problems when I made them the gods they were never meant to be. The fact that I was to have no other gods before Him was for my good and the good of others. His "jealousy" was to have us love Him first so that we might have life and love to the fullest. Now it made sense. I hit my knees and asked forgiveness for making Jerry my God. Then I went to my husband and asked his forgiveness for expecting perfection out of him at all times and expecting him to meet my every need. I told him I had put him in God's place, but I was letting him go to love and serve God without my impossible expectations. Our house sold for good two days later.

We built a lovely little house on the loathsome lot and I put my grandchildren's names on the stair risers going up to their room. We were happy there, but my husband's health took a turn for the worse with spinal stenosis, a failed surgery and complications from his prostate cancer. I talked him into retiring, and after he retired, he wanted to build another house! It had been thirty-three years since I had given houses to God. I was tired of them, but I had pledged to go with my husband's decisions about houses. We moved twenty minutes out of town to a resort neighborhood called Brasada Ranch. It was quiet, peaceful and beautiful. We made numerous, good Christian friends there and I was so grateful.

Soon after settling in, we were building a custom home for difficult people. I started to shut down. I couldn't keep up this constant building. It was a nightmare for both of us, especially Jerry. Some aspects of the building process took too long, the buyers kept changing their minds and making changes that set the timeline back. Toward the end of finishing the house, the buyers, with their attorney, tried to force us into letting them move in without paying us. Of course we didn't let them, and the animosity that created was very stressful. The good that came out of that experience was Jerry hanging up his tool belt and apologizing to me. Our building days were over.

It has been thirty-six years since I gave up houses and I've had nothing but houses since. We have packed up our belongings and moved sixteen times during those years. God has provided for our family and taught us innumerable lessons through those houses. He gave my husband a second career and provided financially for our six children. Those houses paid for prom dresses, sports fees, wheelchairs, ten sets of orthodontic braces, summer camps, college tuition and weddings. He gave us great vacations together and gave us many friends in many places as we moved about. He taught us to trust Him implicitly in good times and in bad. He used houses to bring my husband back to Him in a mighty way and he saved him from my perfectionistic expectations. He used houses to make us financially wealthy and He used them to take away half of our net worth. He used them to improve our marriage. He taught me why I may not have any other gods before Him; it is for my happiness and the happiness of others. He taught me that houses come and go and they are not important. He taught me to keep my eyes always upon Him and look forward to my permanent house in heaven, the one He is building for me.

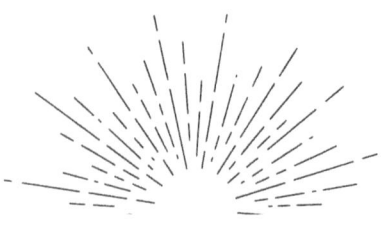

SIXTEEN

Devastating Loss

On my knees, every morning for a year, I prayed God would save my son. In answer, He took him home to Himself. My love for Him increased tenfold.

It was a very upsetting Christmas. That statement is wrong in so many ways. How can Christmas be upsetting? It can and it is in many households each year. It had never been in ours, but this year it was. Trying to understand how things fell apart, I wondered, *Did I elevate the children above Him? Did I try too hard to control the outcome? Were there just too many imperfect people with inner struggles all together in one close space?*

We had moved to Brasada Ranch and had extra bedrooms, bathrooms, a view of all the Cascade Mountains and the Ranch had fun Christmas activities planned for families. We wanted to share all this with our children and grandchildren, so I began inviting them to come home. All together there would be twenty-one of us celebrating. All the children jumped at the chance to spend Christmas with us; all except Joe. He was swamped with work in Montana and couldn't take the time off. He and his precious daughter Chloe would have to pass.

The closer we came to Christmas, the heavier my heart grew with missing Joe. I shared my distress with my husband and we decided to offer Joe plane tickets home so he would only be absent from work for three days. I called him and he declined our offer. A few minutes later, the phone rang and it was Joe. He and Chloe were coming! I booked the flights and sent him the itinerary.

Everyone arrived. Two daughters had homes near us and the other four children and their families stayed at our house. Uncle Joe and Chloe were introduced to the two newest babies in our family. It was a wonderful time filled with love. I had made food ahead of time so I could enjoy everyone. We went on sleigh rides, went ice skating and had breakfast with Santa Claus. The grandchildren were having a great time.

I wanted to do something special for our adult children, so I put money in each of their stockings so they could go out to the Ranch House together on Christmas evening before Joe had to fly home. All the grandchildren would stay home with us.

When our children arrived home from the Ranch House, something was wrong. Tension in the room was palpable. I gathered that things had been said, judged and over-reacted to. A comment was overheard in the kitchen, feelings were hurt, more over-reaction, more comments, including one I made out of panic and frustration, and all hell broke loose. Need I say, alcohol had been consumed by all? We had become increasingly concerned over the last couple of years about the frequency and amount of two of our children's drinking. My husband talked to Joe about his drinking the next morning before we took him to the airport. Joe remained closed off and looked at me with frustration when I offered him breakfast. He didn't respond to my hug when he left for the airport with Chloe. He was just silent.

After Christmas, I was devastated deep in my soul. Every single morning, without fail, I began my day by lifting up my Joe and literally begging God to save him. *Father, please save my Joe and bring him to you.* I knew God wanted to save him, so I knew I was praying in His will. I called and texted Joe, left messages of love that were never returned. I knew Joe was struggling with issues in his life but he was also playing and coaching hockey, was working too many hours and loved his time with Chloe. I just kept lifting him up every single morning for God's blessing and ultimate salvation.

The months passed. Joe was scheduled to come home in the summer to wire a house Jerry was building. I was so anxious to see him but the house had setbacks, wasn't ready to wire and my father passed away in July. Joe wasn't able to travel home for the funeral service. I made plans to visit him in Montana in August, but Julie's service dog began failing. Her beautiful Teanne was fourteen years old and had cancer in her head. We couldn't travel to Montana with her and I couldn't leave her and Julie when Teanne was dying. Sweet Teanne died on August fifteenth and by the end of the month I again wanted to head to Montana. My husband said Joe would be home to do the electrical in October, so I waited again, still praying every morning, *God please save him.*

October came and the house still wasn't ready for wiring. I was beyond frustrated. I rented a big house on the Oregon Coast for Thanksgiving and invited our family, because the Oregon Coast was Joe's favorite place. He didn't come. He did comment on his sister's social media posts, so he was thinking about us. He was still coming during the next two months to wire the house Jerry was building. *God, please save Joe!*

On the evening of Monday, December 18, 2017 we got a call that Joe was in the hospital in Missoula. He had been admitted that morning. The emergency room doctor who cared for him was one of his hockey teammates. She told him he was really sick and she was going to put him on a respirator and into a coma to save his life. Before she inserted the respirator, Joe looked up into her eyes and said, "Tell Chloe I love her."

Joe had told a friend he wasn't feeling well on Thursday evening after hockey practice. By Friday, he was too sick to work and called Chloe's mother to ask if Chloe could stay with her a couple more days until he was well. Sunday, he went to Urgent Care and Joe rarely went to see a doctor, so I know he was desperate.

The physician said, "This is the flu. I've seen five cases today."

He ordered an X-ray and sent Joe home! Joe coughed up blood all night long. Early the next morning, he got to the emergency room and was put on the respirator. The Urgent Care called his phone to tell him he had pneumonia. Too little too late. He should have been sent straight to the hospital emergency room the day before. *God, please save my boy.*

After getting the call on Monday evening, we were in shock. My husband was scheduled for a long-awaited surgery the next day. By early morning we were up and getting ready to drive to Missoula. I had checked airline flights but none of them could get us to our Joe sooner and I had to take Julie's medical equipment; too difficult on an airplane. Jerry cancelled his surgery, showered and headed out on the ten-hour drive to Missoula. I showered Julie, packed the van with equipment and suitcases and was ready to go when Jerry called. Joe was being life flighted to Salt Lake City. He had been through a rough night in the hospital and needed to be put on a machine that wasn't available in Missoula. The hospital called around and Salt Lake was the closest that had an available machine. Jerry changed course and headed to Salt Lake City. Julie and I were a couple hours behind him.

Our four other children were now trying to get to their brother, too. Molly found a plane ticket to get to Salt Lake that afternoon and Jerry could pick her up at the airport on his way to the hospital. Heidi and Jennifer booked tickets for early the next morning. Tommy and his wife Ally were in

Europe and they made arrangements to fly home.

As Julie and I sped down the highway on the ten-hour drive to Salt Lake, we prayed for angels around our car. Angels to speed our way and keep us safe. We stopped twice for gas and to use the bathroom. We had water in the car and no appetite for food. Our angels cleared the road for us. No one slowed us down. We weren't pulled over for speeding even though I drove well over the speed limit the entire way. All I could see as I drove was my beautiful boy, alone in the night, coughing up blood. My beautiful boy chilled, weak and so terribly sick. My beautiful boy in a coma, on a respirator, loaded on an airplane, trying to live. Julie and I prayed without ceasing and our mantra was *please save him*.

We made it to the University hospital in Salt Lake City in eight and a half hours. We found Jerry and Molly in a waiting area near Joe's room. It had taken hours for Joe to reach the hospital. The weather in Missoula was dangerous for flying so he had waited hours on the plane just to take off. He had coded twice during the day; once on the flight to the hospital and again in the Emergency Room when he was transferred off the plane. He had been taken for a procedure to try and get pulses back into his legs and was hooked up to machines for his heart, lungs and kidneys. When he returned from the procedure, there were no pulses in his legs. We had come to say goodbye.

We washed, donned gowns and finally saw Joe. I had never loved anyone as much as I loved him at that moment. Jerry, Julie, Molly and I surrounded him, touched him, talked to him and prayed over him. Joe was close to all his siblings but Julie and Molly, our youngest and identical twins, were the introverts along with Joe in our family. They understood each other and had a special bond. Molly, our NICU nurse, looked over his chart, read the blood test results and all the rest of the medical information. She looked at me with sad eyes. I asked her if Joe was dying, even though I knew the answer. She told us with those test results, Joe wouldn't come back.

We continued to talk to Joe and pray. We told him we would watch out for his Chloe and make sure she had everything she needed. We prayed that God's will be done in the short time we had and in eternity. We told our boy just how wonderful he was and how very much we loved him.

At two o'clock in the morning, Joe's nurse informed us that he had no pulses in his arms. He was dying one piece at a time. I conferred with Molly and she told me that Joe could still feel pain and would suffer more if we kept him on the machines. I found his nurse and told her it was time to unhook him.

We had time to say our goodbyes. Jerry and I laid hands on him, thanked God for the treasure he was, the privilege of raising him, learning from him and we released him back to his Creator. I held him close and recited "Good Night Moon" to him from memory. We had read that book together every night before bed during his toddlerhood. We both knew it by heart.

Joe's medical team came in and unhooked our boy from all the machines he was on. Our sweet Joey took his last few bloody breaths at 4 am on December 20, 2017. He was thirty-eight years old and had died from influenza B in only five days. The hardest thing I have ever done was to walk away.

Shock set in, a shock that would last for months. Tommy lived in Salt Lake City at that time. He was on his way home from Europe, so we went to his house, found his key and let ourselves in. We lay down on empty beds to grieve.

Early the next morning, Jerry booked a ticket home for Molly and took her to the airport. Her three-month old baby girl had the flu and was very sick. I was in a fog but needed to take care of Joe's body and getting him home. I prayed for guidance and called a five-star service for cremation I found on the internet. God was with me. The young mother (I could hear her children in the background) who answered my call was a rep for the business. She was kind, compassionate and committed to helping me. She arranged to have Joe's body transferred to a funeral home she believed was the best in the city. She followed up with the funeral home and called me back. Because it was December 20 and the Christmas holiday was upon them, the funeral home couldn't do the cremation until after Christmas. They had others scheduled ahead of Joe. She told me they would mail his ashes to us. I totally fell apart on the phone. I told her between sobs that I wouldn't leave Utah without my son, and my four daughters and nine grandchildren were coming to our house for Christmas. She said to hang in there and she would call me back.

During that long day, my friend Peggy and my sister-in-law Connie both called me. They each had received a scripture from God about Joe. They both quoted me the same scripture!

"For the LORD sees not as man sees; for man looks at the outward appearance, but the LORD looks at the heart." 1 Samuel 16:7b.

The message from God was given and confirmed. He had my Joe!

The next day, on December 21st, my wonderful advocate called me back to tell me the funeral home had moved Joe up on the list and his cremation would take place the next day. I was immensely grateful but another hurdle presented itself. I received a call the following morning, again from my advocate. She had called the hospital three times and still didn't have a death certificate. The day before, the physician couldn't find the paperwork and just went home. She was getting nowhere calling the hospital staff and if a death certificate wasn't delivered by 3pm, there would be no cremation. She asked for my help.

I called the hospital. I stated my problem and was transferred to someone in charge. Through tears, sobs and anger, I told the supervisor how my son had died and how I had fought to take him home by Christmas.

I finally said, "Can you really tell me that in all your big hospital, in two and a half days' time, there is no physician who can sign the death certificate of a beloved thirty-eight-year-old who died in your care?"

Ten minutes later our precious advocate called and told me they had the death certificate. That was the last time of many I advocated for my son.

It was fitting that I had to go to bat for him one last time.

On December 23, we were able to pick up Joe's ashes at 3 pm. His ashes rode home with me on the front passenger's seat of our van. We were driving in tandem because we had two cars. Our plan was to drive straight through to home, but by the time we reached Boise I couldn't keep my eyes open. I signaled my husband to pull over and he took us to the closest hotel. We fell into bed, me holding Joe's ashes, and slept for a few hours in our clothes. We trekked the last five hours and arrived home with Joe on Christmas Eve. We were joined by our daughters, their spouses and grandchildren. It was a sad time for all of us, but shock numbed the pain we shared and the grandchildren brought us joy.

Shortly after Joe died, my youngest sister Terri called me and asked if she could please take care of Joe's celebration of life. She would fly out from Pennsylvania and handle everything. What a gift! During these days, I was in a daze. My husband couldn't cry with me and that was a problem. Julie was stoic but shattered. Joe had championed her for her entire life. This was another deep and shattering loss for her. The nights were brutal for me. I couldn't turn off the pain. I couldn't sleep. I had begged God every morning for a year to save my boy, but not like this. This wasn't my plan. I'd had numerous ideas of how He could save Joe and this wasn't one of them. None of them included taking him home to heaven. My faith didn't waiver, but I was crushed by this answer. I begged God every dark, sleepless night to let me know my boy was ok. One night I finally took Joe's ashes off my bedside table and held them tight to my heart. I slept.

Terri flew in from Pennsylvania very early in the morning of December 28th. When I quietly left my bedroom at 5 AM., I found her sitting on my couch. I flew into her arms and we hugged and cried together.

She said, "Linda, I have something I need to tell you."

She had gone to church on Christmas Eve and after communion went back to her pew and knelt down to pray. Something unexpected happened. She was given a vision. She saw hands reaching out. She looked up to see whose hands they were and saw a bright, blinding light. She looked back to where the hands were reaching and there was Joe. He had his amazing smile and he radiated with the light. The vision vanished. God, in His holy mercy, had answered my plea through my sister. He showed me that He had my Joe and Joe was surrounded by and filled with love.

DEVASTATING LOSS

The celebration of life was to be held on December 30th, just ten days after we said good bye to our son. We sent plane tickets to Joe's daughter, Chloe, and her mother so they could be with us. My sister took care of all the details for that day. It was held at Shevlin Park Hall, a beautiful setting by a small lake in Bend, Oregon. It had a capacity of one-hundred fifty people. There had been no obituary published and Joe had lived away for nineteen years, so we thought the venue was the right size. There was Standing Room Only. At least two-hundred people poured into that hall. Joe's friends just kept coming. Teammates and friends from high school came by plane, bus and car to honor him. Family friends and coaches from his youth travelled over snowy mountains to be there. The love that filled that room was incredible.

I wanted to share about my son. I shared about his name Joseph, meaning increasing faithfulness, and how my hope for him was that he would become a strong witness for God. I shared about how he struggled to fit into a world he didn't understand. He didn't understand evil because his soul was good. In the end, he increased our faith and taught us important lessons by the way he lived.

Our son Tommy spoke for his siblings. He shared how Joe had helped each brother and sister many times over, fixing the electrical system in their homes, never expecting or accepting payment for all the work he did. He shared how he always called Joe if he was in trouble or needed to talk and Joe listened and gave him sound, loving advice. He told everyone how Joe brought the fun to every gathering and how Joe's message on every graduation quilt I made for each sibling was always the most insightful. He shared with everyone how Joe's empty space among the siblings fractured them. He expressed their deep love for their brother.

We asked one friend to share about Joe. Hector Samkow was huge in Joe's life. They were very much alike and Joe had loved him since he was a toddler. Up until Joe's death, he would stop by to visit Hector just to talk. Hector, in his very humble way, spoke about meeting Joe when he was one year old. He talked about the years our families spent together loving each other. He called our home the house of love and we had told him that love came from God. He shared about a gift Joe had made for him when Joe was young. It was a wood sign that said "Hector's Workshop" and twenty-five years later it was still hanging in his workshop.

Joe's sister Heidi had put together a wonderful DVD of Joe's life in pictures and music. After watching it, we were able to hear stories about Joe from his friends while sharing food and drink. As guests began leaving, one young man approached me.

"Mrs. Hackenbruck ma'am, I don't know if you remember me. My name is Josh Gage and I want to share with you how Joe changed my life."

He told me he became a father at age fifteen, a sophomore in high school, and that fact changed his status, friends and how he was perceived. Joe arrived at school the next year and befriended Josh. Josh invited Joe to his home where he lived with his parents and three siblings. Joe really liked his family and his friendship with them blossomed. They remained good friends into college when Josh sought Joe's advice about joining the service. Joe told him he would be a great leader and would be successful there. Josh told me Joe always encouraged and believed in him.

Josh looked me in the eye and said, "Mrs. Hackenbruck, I now work at the Pentagon. I'm married and have three children. That's all because of Joe."

Josh Gage had flown from Washington, D.C. to honor Joe and share his story with Joe's momma. I hadn't known anything about that story. I was humbled, grateful and very proud of my son's loving heart.

Another celebration of Joe's life took place in Missoula three weeks later. Again, standing room only. Joe was very loved by his friends, hockey teammates and clients he worked for. One of his teammates told us that she fell in practice and broke her foot. Joe carried her to his car, took her to the hospital and stayed with her until she was released. He took her home, got her settled and returned every day to help her. Another teammate told us his wife was very shy but wanted to try playing hockey. Joe heard about it, befriended her, encouraged her to join his team and they became fast friends. She couldn't attend his memorial because she was still too shaken up over his death. Joe was loved at Chloe's Catholic school where he donated his time and work expertise. So many people loved him. He may not have become a pillar of the Church but he had become a pillar of Jesus' command that we love one another. Joe had walked a path of service and love.

After coming home from Missoula, the world kept turning, but I didn't. I still couldn't sleep without Joe's ashes pressed tightly to my heart. I cried out to God for help. He sent Joe back to me in a dream. It was as vivid as real life. In the dream, I was talking to my younger sister. Our two families were going rafting together. She told me that her ex-husband had asked Joe to watch their grandchildren so Joe wouldn't be able to go. She said she didn't want to interfere with her ex but she was upset by his actions and thought I should know. I told her I would call Joe and talk to him about it. I'd tell him he didn't have to babysit. I got my phone out and started to dial when I became aware of someone approaching behind me. I turned and there was Joe, so real and whole.

I said, "Joe, I was just going to call you."

He answered, "Now you don't have to. I'm here Momma."

He hugged me. So real. A Joe hug, his arms surrounding me, his feel, his smell, all that love. I woke up. I was crying. I wanted to go back to him but I couldn't get back. God had let me see him, hold him one last time; one last goodbye.

Even after that gift of a last goodbye, I'm ashamed to say, my anger and despair continued. I'm even more ashamed to say I directed that anger and despair at my husband. Part of the problem was he couldn't grieve with me. I'm emotional and feel deeply. He's steady, rock solid and keeps feelings inside. These differences had worked well in our marriage but they were destroying us now. I needed him to cry with me, to talk about Joe, to rant against God for saving our son by taking him. Jerry couldn't cry with me. He truly felt that God taking Joe was the best because that was His answer to my fervent prayers. It was His will. He wouldn't share my anger, so I turned it on him and I threw out lies. Satan had now entered into my grief, but he wasn't going to win.

    I reminded Jerry of all the times he wasn't there for Joe when Joe was growing up; how he spent his time coaching with other people's sons instead of his own son; how he favored Tommy over Joe. I accused him of having no feelings, no depth inside of him. I continued on to what a horrible husband he had been, how he left me alone most of the time to handle everything with our six children. I mentioned divorce and ended with how much he had hurt me. After all that, what did my husband do? He walked over to me, took me into his arms, held me tight against his chest and said, "I love you." He saw and heard my pain and countered it with his unconditional love and he healed me.

    I continued to talk to God and Joe every day. I wanted to honor Joe's life with mine in some way. Through prayer, I discerned two things Joe wanted. He was so close to his sister Julie and even though we had spent thirty-three years giving her the best care we could, it seemed like there was something we were missing. As I prayed with Jerry and listened for God's voice, we became aware that living out of town in a mostly retirement community was not the best situation for a thirty-three-year-old young woman. After much prayer, we moved back to the city where Julie's twin sister lived so Julie could have time with her sister and a richer life.

The second way of honoring Joe was more personal. He had adored his father and would get angry with me if I said anything that could be considered critical about him. I had many defenses for my complaints and criticisms, but the truth was my behavior was wrong and my son had called me out on it. To honor Joe, I vowed to love his father with acceptance and encouragement, not criticism. I have not been perfect in this vow, but the blessings that have come out of this tribute are innumerable. Through obedience in my marriage to God's will and Joe's heart's desire, God has restored the love of our youth. The scars and hurts of forty-eight years together have all but disappeared. We are so happy and I can feel Joe smiling.

Eventually, something else happened that makes no sense in this world. I had always had trouble understanding how I could love God with all my heart, soul, mind and strength when I had my husband, children and grandchildren taking up some of that space. After Joe's death, instead of being filled with resentment toward God, I finally truly loved him with all my heart, soul, mind and strength. How could losing Joe, who I loved so desperately, make me love God more? Losing my son made me realize not only in my mind but also in my heart that there is no love without God, not even for those I hold most dear. We all come from God and are returning to Him in His time. The only true love I can live on this earth is His love through me. By loving Him with all my heart, soul, mind and strength, I can give true love to those I hold most dear and fulfill my purpose on this earth. By giving Him all, I have more to give others. This surrender has deeply changed my days.

It has been five years now since Joe was taken home to Jesus. I've learned that time and space are an illusion. Joe is still here as well as "there." I feel his presence every day and knowing he lives fills me with so much joy. The Holy Spirit always connects us and when I finally walk into the light and love, Joe will be waiting.

SEVENTEEN

One More House: Julie's Prayer

*Who besides God could possibly meet every
need on our impossible list?*

After Joe's death, the months slowly passed and we talked about moving again. Brasada Ranch was a dream spot but our dreams were going in another direction. Julie needed more than Brasada offered her. She needed contact with her twin sister and activity a larger city could provide. Jerry and I prayed and talked every morning about the pros and cons of moving. It always boiled down to Julie. Julie wanted to move close to her sister but I could see she was anxious about something. I sat down with her and explained that the move was not a done deal. We were a family, all three of us equally important in decisions. Did she want to stay at Brasada? Julie found her voice and her fear poured out. She wanted to move close to Molly but she was afraid to leave the accessible home we built for her.

The new home would need to be one level with wide hallways and rooms large enough for a motorized wheelchair to travel around in them. Julie's bedroom needed space as well as an open closet to install pull-out baskets for her clothes. Most important was her bathroom accessibility, toilet, vanity and roll in shower. We would need a three-car garage with room to lower the ramp on Julie's wheelchair van so she could get in and out safely. The house would need to be in a safe neighborhood with sidewalks so she could get out and walk her service dog. And all of this would need to be within ten minutes of Molly's home.

Life in a wheelchair is tough; the practicalities overwhelming. Because Julie was joyful, positive, funny, kind and forever uncomplaining, it was so easy to forget what she faced each day. I told her if she wanted to move, her dad and I would make sure our new home would work for her. The promise was made and I alone would have to fulfill it. Or would I?

We put our house up for sale. We had a budget to sell and a budget to buy. We would not build again.

ONE MORE HOUSE: JULIE'S PRAYER

Those days were over. The task ahead appeared to be the impossible dream. We would need a miracle!

After spending a month glued to the Zillow website watching homes come and go, Julie informed me that I had little faith because I was trying to control everything. Of course, she was right. I sat right down with her and we made a list of everything we needed and hoped for in a home. I even added lots of windows for light and enough room to gather our large family together. Julie and I prayed over that list and gave it up to God. I'll admit, I backslid a few times when she caught me on the computer looking at Zillow. She reminded me we had prayed and left it in God's hands. I wondered if my daughter's faith might move this mountain. Four long months passed and we trusted and waited for our miracle.

Over a weekend in October, Julie stayed with her sister so Jerry and I could attend a fundraiser three hours away in Portland. During the fundraiser, I received a call from our realtor telling us we had just received a generous offer on our house. We were so excited and quickly accepted the offer. The next morning, my phone dinged just after we had left our hotel and headed home. It was an alert from Zillow showing a new house had just hit the market. This was strange because I had never received an alert from Zillow before. I immediately looked up the house and it was a one level home in a nice neighborhood. We turned the car around, drove back and found the home. It was beautiful from the outside, a little over our price range, but not much. In the car on our way home, I called a real estate friend and we scheduled a showing for three days later.

We met up with our realtor and entered the house, tape measure in hand. Our mission here was simple. Would this house work for Julie? We stepped into an entryway lighted by a large crystal chandelier. It was impressive but overwhelming to me. I am a simple person and our homes had always reflected that. Putting my feelings aside, Julie came to the forefront. Could she get into this house? Steps led up to the front door and the garage had four steps going into the home. A paved path travelled from the driveway around to the back kitchen door, but in the rain or snow it wouldn't be practical for Julie's wheelchair. Jerry measured the three-car garage and said we had just enough room to build a semi-steep ramp for Julie to use to enter the house. It was either a ramp or a lift in the garage. Ramps don't break down, so that would be our choice.

We moved on to the interior of the house. It had an open floor plan, wide hallways, huge kitchen

ONE MORE HOUSE: JULIE'S PRAYER

with room for a wheelchair to move around the island and huge windows in every room. The master bedroom wouldn't be an issue but Julie's would be. Both of the two remaining bedrooms were very large. One of them had a double wall closet, perfect for Julie. The only problem we encountered in the house was the Jack and Jill bathroom between the two extra bedrooms. The sinks and toilet/tub were divided by a wall and Julie's chair would not fit in either side. Out came the tape measure. If we removed the wall in the bathroom, pulled out the tub and replaced it with a roll-in shower, adapted one-half of the vanity for a wheelchair to roll under and widened the door into the bathroom, it would work! There was just enough room for a wheelchair to enter and turn around.

The house met everything on Julie's and my list and, depending on a stop light, it was only 3-5 minutes from Molly. It also had more than we asked for: wood floors and sturdy carpet, crown moldings in every room, beautiful wainscoting, and lovely light fixtures. God always gives more than we ask because He loves us. Six weeks later, we moved in. Julie's ramp was built and her bathroom remodel started.

Over five years later, I'm still in awe of God's concern and involvement in our personal needs and problems. Who besides God could possibly meet every need on our impossible list for a house? His deep love and care for Julie is amazing. He richly rewarded and increased her faith by again using houses. The sincere prayer I made in tears and on my knees thirty-seven years before was not forgotten. God honors a humble heart, a heart filled with love and trust in Him.

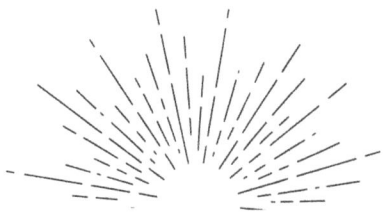

EIGHTEEN
The Light and the Love

Seeing Jesus! We had never been alone.

The thought of counseling was terrifying to me but I needed it badly. I felt deep down if I turned everything over to God, he would heal my fears.

"Perfect love casts out fear." 1 John 4:18.

I knew in my heart this was true, but I was still filled with irrational fear. If one of my children was driving home over the Cascades from university, and was half an hour late, I went into a panic. I was so convinced they had been in an accident, I could barely function. Fear was my constant companion. If I wasn't in control of a situation, someone might get hurt.

My husband and our family physician sent me off to counseling. I met with a calm, caring and skilled counselor. She told me she was looking at a woman who seemed very nervous and about to jump out of her chair. She had me do deep breathing with her until I could calm down. Then we got to work.

She told me my fearfulness was due to PTSD. My physician had shared with her my toddlerhood experience of watching my mother try to kill my father. That was my earliest memory and I was two and a half years old. My sisters, who were four and five years old, were with me in the dining room of our tiny house. About ten feet away, my mother was screaming and crying, trying to stab my father with a butcher knife. He was blocking her arm to stop her. I can still see the room, table, expressions, everything. I was screaming in terror and my five-year- old sister pulled me to the wall and stood in front of me. The memory stops.

With my counselor's guidance, my two-year-old self began to heal. I learned about PTSD and how it affects a brain, specifically my brain that was still quickly developing at age two. I learned where my fear originated and why my brain perpetuated it. I discovered the source of my perfectionism, my need to keep everyone happy and safe all the time, to fix problems so they wouldn't escalate. She showed me why I couldn't watch violence, real or make-believe, why I so fiercely protected my children and other children, too. She told me

I had been a very intelligent and strong toddler to form an unconscious plan to keep myself and others around me safe. My young self knew that if I was perfect, I wouldn't set my mother off and get into trouble. If I kept everyone happy and solved problems quickly, they would be safe, too. On the outside I excelled at life, but on the inside my fear and insecurity had taken its toll.

My counselor worked with me on issues she saw as connected to the PTSD. She asked me why I was afraid to set boundaries with my adult children. After considering her question, I quietly answered,

"Because I'm afraid they won't love me."

It shocked me to hear my answer and I started to cry.

My counselor showed me that the little girl who made herself perfect, fixed everything and asked for nothing was still inside and still afraid. The love I had received was based on behavior and performance, not just on me being me. I'd never received unconditional love, and I couldn't fathom being loved if I didn't perform perfectly. Over the next few months, I became aware of how PTSD and my faulty belief system had affected every area of my life, but especially my relationships with my husband and children. With my counselor's help, my fear lost much of its hold on me and I was able to love more authentically.

During the years that followed, I saw three more counselors. All were helpful. One helped me open up in my marriage, and another explained the physiology and psychology of complex PTSD: my mom trying to kill my dad, Julie's seizure and imminent death in the NICU, and watching my son Joe die. She used diagrams and research to show me why my experiences were so imbedded in my brain and why they so easily controlled my behavior. The third and last counselor guided me to true healing.

I went to her because life circumstances were dragging me down, robbing me of my joy. During the first session, she took my history. During the second session, we listed the issues I needed to tackle. She practiced EMDR, a therapy method used to heal memories. I was to relive the memory while focusing on her finger moving back and forth in a steady motion. This would let me acknowledge the memory, see it in a new light of healing, and put it on a "shelf" in my brain where it would be contained. She asked me which memory I would like to start with at our next session. I chose the one that woke me up the most often during the night; watching Julie having a full body seizure that stopped her heart and lungs while I was praying over her.

The day of my next counseling appointment, I

THE LIGHT AND THE LOVE

stayed with my grandchildren while my daughter Jennifer was at work. When she arrived home, perceptive as always, she asked me if something was wrong. I confided to her my fear of going to counseling and reliving Julie's seizure in the NICU. I didn't want to relive it. Jennifer told me she would be praying for me as I headed to counseling. When I arrived, my counselor explained the EMDR process to me again. She asked me to describe the memory I was going to revisit. I saw my mottled, puffy Julie struggling to breathe. I saw a seizure beginning and her entire little body rising six inches off the bed as her arms and legs flung stiffly out, and then her body landed. Her appearance had changed and her body was too soft and floppy. The alarms on her machines were going off, a nurse was calling the doctor and it took him so long to get to us. The nurse started CPR and the doctor finally intubated Julie.

 I was shaking with fear as my counselor started the rhythm with her finger and I faded back to face the demons, but the demons weren't there. I was back in the NICU watching myself standing and praying by the side of Julie's bed, but I wasn't alone. Standing at the end of her little open bed, facing her, was a white-robed figure covered in light and radiating love, both directed solely at Julie. The light was intense and beautiful and I could feel the healing love go through me.

We had never been alone. A doctor's free will and pride had hurt my precious daughter but Jesus had never left us. His healing light and love were saving her life as she suffered that seizure.

The rhythm of EMDR stopped and I came back to the present. My counselor quickly grabbed paper to write down the first thing I said.

"He loved that baby even more than I did and I loved her a whole lot."

I told her Jesus was there with us in the NICU. I told her about the light and the love, the beautiful light that covered my baby and the incredible, healing love that filled me. I never wanted to leave it. I never wanted to leave Him. I was gifted this experience of seeing and feeling Jesus three months before my son Joe died of the flu. Looking back, God in his incredible mercy and love was preparing me to let my son go. When Joe died, I knew without a doubt where he was going. He was going into the light and into the love.

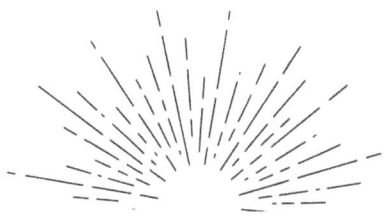

CONCLUSION

From the Heart

At the end of our lives, He is all that matters.

Now the stories are written down, but they are far from over. As long as I live the stories will continue, because God and His deep love are so great. I've drawn close to Him and He has remained faithful throughout my life. It has not been an easy life and it isn't easy today. Jesus didn't promise easy at any time during his ministry. My life has been full of fear, anger, despair and confusion. Each time I drew close to God and trusted Him with my circumstances, He turned them into acceptance, joy, humility, wisdom and even the ability to love what I thought was unlovable. He has given me more and more of the heart of his son Jesus. In doing so He has filled my life with ever more love and joy, even in the toughest of circumstances.

The world does not know Jesus, but many of us do. He came to reveal the Father and He revealed Him to perfection. He showed us that God is wise, humble, patient, powerful, healing, all-knowing and loving in all circumstances. He revealed to us that God values eternal qualities, He loves all people and will teach His ways to those who seek Him with a true and humble heart. He showed us that God is willing to undergo the worst of all suffering for the chance to save those He created, and turn them to Himself. He revealed to us a God who is the same yesterday, today and tomorrow.

As Christians, we have a direct line to God through Jesus and a Holy Spirit who dwells within to teach and guide us. Our prayers are heard and our faith brings them straight to the Father's heart. At a young age I found Jesus. He led me to Himself and kept me close. He welcomed me into the life of love, trust, obedience and faith and blessed me beyond anything I could have imagined. He will do the same for all His children as they give their lives and trust to him.

I have shared with you my miracles, springing up out of faith and trust, answers to prayer from a generous, loving Father, always giving more than we know to ask for. Our Father, who intimately interacts with us, takes what we surrender to Him and turns it into something beautiful.

If we live one year or one hundred years, life is short. We are but a speck in eternity and yet God loves each one of us infinitely. He is seeking each of us and waiting for our response to His call. The only way to really know Him is to draw close to Him, talk to Him and trust Him. He only makes sense to those who truly know Him, and at the end of our lives, He is all that matters.

We can argue with the world forever about the reality of God and our arguments will end in frustration. The only proof of God is the proof we live. No one can discount it or deny it. It is our lives and our love rather than our arguments that reveal the Father, Son and Holy Spirit to the world. Why do I live my life to follow Jesus and love the Father? Because I stepped out in trust and found Them to be faithful and true in every way. I found a deep life, full of love, joy and grace abundant. I have shared my stories with you, and they are my powerful proof.

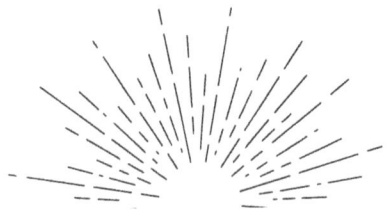

Acknowledgements

I would like to thank my husband for insisting I publish my stories, because they might help "just one person;" my children for living with an imperfect mother and loving her anyway; my sister, Mara, for spending hours editing my stories with her brilliant mind and for loving and encouraging me; the precious women in my Resurrection Bible study, who heard my stories and said they made a difference; and the blessed Holy Spirit who told me to write the miracles down and waited patiently, for fifteen years, until I finished them.

Milton Keynes UK
Ingram Content Group UK Ltd.
UKHW030134021124
450424UK00006B/833